ENDORSEME

Nothing, and I do mean nothing, excites me more than the testimonies of an outpouring of the Holy Spirit. *True Stories of Azusa Street* is a perfect example. They cause my heart to burn for the "more" found on the pages of Scripture and recorded in history.

This book by Tommy Welchel and Michelle P. Griffith is the sequel to *They Told Me Their Stories*. Known as the last living link to the Azusa Street Awakening, Tommy had the great privilege of sitting at the feet and hearing the stories of those who experienced the outpouring firsthand. This record of miracles from God's goodness is absolutely stunning.

Prepare to be encouraged and challenged in your faith as you read the record of an awakening that is still being felt today. More importantly, prepare to hunger for *more* in your lifetime.

BILL JOHNSON
Pastor, Bethel Church, Redding CA
Author of *When Heaven Invades Earth* and *Hosting the Presence*

It did not take very long before I was excited about this book and it's great story. I know you will be inspired. It can happen again -- even greater because the time is short. Let's get our faith up and be inspired for a fresh outpouring of God's Spirit.

GLORIA COPELAND
Kenneth Copeland Ministires

We are in the year 2013. It is no coincidence that this book you hold is being written and unleashed. In 1909, William Seymour, the great revival pioneer and father of the Azusa Street Movement, prophesied along with Maria Woodworth-Etter, the mighty healing revivalist, that in 100 years a revival, far greater in power and influence than Azusa Street would be sent from heaven again. It's 2013! We're in the 100-year period! It's time. Could this book be the catalyst for this prophesied heavenly invasion to be released? Read afresh the stories of Azusa Street that still go on and become an instrument in this next heavenly invasion.

Lou Engle
Co-Founder and President of TheCall

There is power in the testimony. Tommy Welchel has recorded many of the outstanding miracles of the Azusa Street Revival. This generation will capture the impartation of this major move of God's Spirit. It will radiate from the pages.

Sid Roth
Host, *It's Supernatural!*

I have learned over the years that God always has His witnesses. Tommy Welchel is a witness to the Azusa Glory. He carries that anointing as it was transmitted to him with each Azusa story he absorbed. Together Tommy and Michelle in *True Stories of the Miracles of Azusa Street and Beyond* have captured that anointing combined with today's anointing for each one of us for God's glorious finale! God bless you, Tommy and Michelle, for obeying the Lord and compiling this vital information for such a time as this!

Billye Brim
Billye Brim Ministries

It is with great pleasure that I recommend to you *True Stories of the Miracles of Azusa Street and Beyond*. I have always loved revival history, and have been blessed by reading these stories. It is a desire of mine to always see more, and the stories in this book have inspired me to ask for more. They are a chapter of our spiritual heritage in the world today. The stories of healing that we see here are foreshadows of what God is doing in the world today, and the movements that have started, have come from people being made hungry. The hunger is inspired by stories of what God has done, which inspires the question, why not here? Why not now? The new stories are no exception.

I encourage you, as you read this book to ask God to take your hunger and increase it. To increase your desire to see Him move on the earth today in power.

RANDY CLARK
Global Awakening

"The actions of the forefathers and mothers are a sign to the children" is a common Jewish expression. The testimonies and stories of past generations are so significant because what the Lord does in the past is a sneak preview of what He wants to do in the future. That is why this is one of the more timely and exciting books that I have seen in awhile. What the Lord did in the days of William Seymour and Azusa serves as a reminder and testimony to what He wants to do in even greater measure in our day. These stories will increase your faith for the impossible and will release the supernatural into your life through the power of testimony. May God breathe upon it and cause it to stir revival!

RABBI JASON SOBEL
Founder of FUSION Global
Spiritual Leader of Ascend Malibu Fellowship

TRUE STORIES
of the
MIRACLES *of*
AZUSA
STREET
and BEYOND

Re-live One of the Greatest Outpourings in History
that is Breaking Loose Once Again…

TOMMY WELCHEL
and MICHELLE P. GRIFFITH

Images courtesy of Flower Pentecostal Heritage Center

DESTINY IMAGE® PUBLISHERS, INC.
P.O. Box 310, Shippensburg, PA 17257-0310
"Promoting Inspired Lives."

This book and all other Destiny Image, Revival Press, MercyPlace, Fresh Bread, Destiny Image Fiction, and Treasure House books are available at Christian bookstores and distributors worldwide.

For a U.S. bookstore nearest you, call 1-800-722-6774.
For more information on foreign distributors, call 717-532-3040.
Reach us on the Internet: www.destinyimage.com.

ISBN 13 TP: 978-0-7684-0351-0
ISBN 13 Ebook: 978-0-7684-8481-6

For Worldwide Distribution, Printed in the U.S.A.
23 24 25 26 27 / 28 27 26 25 24

TO THE YOUNG
(And the Child of God in Us All)

You are never too young (or too old) to enter in the Kingdom of God and do God's work.

These stories are about the youth of Azusa Street. These are the children who gave up playing after school to go to the mission and witness and perform miracles, the teenagers who not only healed hundreds but who also went on to start some of the most significant religious movements of our time.

Are you young? Or old? God wants to use you, right here, right now. Get ready!

From left to right:
Brother Anderson, Sister Carney,
Brother Sines, Brother Christopher

Azusa Group (William Seymour is fifth from right.)

Young Sines with parents

ACKNOWLEDGMENTS

"A time to plant and a time to harvest." (ECCLESIASTES 3:2)

Tommy is a storyteller. A storyteller can't talk to a recording device without eyes and ears on the other side of it. We want to thank our "listening audience" whose mere willing presence ushered in the anointing that allowed Tommy to recall and recount the tales in this book. This includes Parish John, Cathy Sandahl, Barbra Chaffee, Carita Boshoff, David Kelly, and Randy and Ana Carranza. Thank you also to our transcriptionist, Colleen Ferraro, who lent listening ears and nimble fingers to hours upon hours of audio recording.

Last, but by no means least, Tommy would like to especially thank his wife of forty-eight years, Marlene, for all her hard work and constant support of this book.

Michelle would like to thank her husband, Marc, for encouraging her to work on this project and always supporting her dreams. She thanks her children, Connor, Victoria and Camryn, who had less of her so that she could put more into this book. Michelle also thanks her mother and father, Frances and Richard Palmieri, who gave her the gift of the knowledge of God in her childhood.

Tommy and Michelle thank *all* who have sown into this book so that many can reap the fruit.

CONTENTS

FOREWORD

God is the magnificent storyteller, and testimony is that which keeps His great stories alive. Not only that, but God's stories are generational in nature. The stories of the past become the stories of the present.

What you are about to read is God's great story of Azusa Street that was, is, and still is to come. Tommy Welchel lived the stories of Azusa Street, and through him, the stories go on, not just told but enacted in this present throbbing moment.

I was swept into this great storyline of Azusa Street in 1984. I read the story of Frank Bartleman's intercessory history as he prayed and fasted in 1905 and recorded the most stirring events that erupted into what we know as the Azusa Street Revival. His stories set me on fire. Moses had a burning bush, but I encountered God in a burning book and heard my name being called. Reading the book, I found myself walking the same streets as Bartleman walked in Pasadena, California. I had tapped into an ancient well and and a glorious father line. Bartleman's promises became mine. I want to pray like that man. I don't just want to read about revival - I want to live in it now. I want my kids to see it. I cried out late one night in '84, "Give me the mantle of Frank Bartleman!"

The following morning a friend came to me and said, "Lou, I had a dream of you last night. In the dream, I saw a big black book and the title said, 'Revival, by Frank Bartleman.'" My friend turned to the inside of the cover of this book, and there was the face of Frank Bartleman. He then said, "His face turned into your face." My whole being exploded with promise. I found my name in the story of Azusa Street and that Frank Bartleman's promises are my promises.

We saw revival in Pasadena from 1994 through 1998. TheCall was born in that revival and hundreds of thousands have gathered to fast and pray for the next outpouring. That dream wasn't about me alone, but a whole generation that would rise up and carry Bartleman's mantle to birth maybe the greatest revival America and the world has ever seen.

During those Pasadena days, I went to Pisgah, and I heard some of those stories of that well, where Tommy Welchel lived and saw the glory of the tongue of fire.

My spirit was drawn to the primordial call of that place where the flame of Azusa Street leapt. I've gone to Sunderland, England, where the Azusa flame leapt and landed on the head of Smith Wigglesworth. In every place the tongue of fire came, God's stories were written and are now retold again to the great grandchildren of William Seymour, C.H. Mason, T. A. Barrett, Smith Wigglesworth, Frank Bartleman, and on and on.

Once again, where the stories are retold, the same spirit of Azusa Street leaps forward. The last chapter has not yet been written. Everything within me screams to be a part of that storyline and, today, in a little coffee cafe in Pasadena, I write this Foreword to a book that will burn across the world and cause Azusa Street to live again and again.

Nine years ago, I left Pasadena on a prayer revival journey across America and the world. Sovereignly, I have been brought back to Pasadena, Bartleman's early prayer ground, and the flame lives in me again as it does in Tommy Welchel. We are in the year 2013, and not by coincidence, this book you hold has been written and is being unleashed. In 1909, William Seymour, the great revival pioneer and father of the Azusa Street Movement prophesied along with Maria Woodworth-Etter, the mighty healing revivalist, that in 100 years, a revival, far greater in power and **influence than Azusa Street** would be sent from heaven again. It's 2013! We are in the 100-year period! It's time!

Could this book be the catalyst for this prophesied heavenly invasion to be released?

My prayer is that the stories told here by a man who saw it, lived and lives it, and is telling the stories again, would be a flame sending forth burning bushes from across the world to those who would take the gospel to the 7,000 unreached people groups that must yet have a witness of the Kingdom before Jesus returns. Let us not waste the anointing on simply experiencing a happy party. Let us take the power of the flaming tongue for the reason it was first sent into that Pentecostal upper room— "You shall receive power when the Holy Spirit comes upon you, and you shall be my witnesses in Jerusalem, Judea and the uttermost parts of the earth."

And maybe for such a time as this, I have come back to L. A. with thousands of others who live here and are moving here to give ourselves to Bartleman's groanings, to birth as he did, the tongue of fire in 2013!

This book documents it clearly. It's more than a good read - it's an invitation into God's final chapter. Will your name be written in the pages of God's heavenly journal? The storyline goes on. Will you be an actor on the stage of history for such a time as this?

Lou Engle
Co-Founder and President of TheCall

PREFACE
by Michelle P. Griffith

*"Heal the sick, raise the dead...
and cast out demons."* (Matthew 10:8a)

AZUSA STREET AND THE SHEKINAH GLORY

If you are reading this book, most likely you are already familiar with the Azusa Street Revival. But for those who are not, 312 Azusa Street, Los Angeles, California, was God's earthly address from April 1906 until November 1909. What do I mean?

The glory of God inhabited this former warehouse and stable in the early years of the twentieth century, releasing creative miracles of healing twenty-four hours a day, seven days a week, for three-and-a-half years. Missing limbs grew out where there were none, eyeballs filled in empty sockets, cancerous growths fell off and lives were restored as the Shekinah Glory filled the building.

To some, *shekinah* is an unfamiliar term. According to rabbinical teaching, the word means "God tents here." The word itself is not biblical, but the Shekinah Glory is found in Scripture. A "cloud" is described throughout Exodus. In Exodus 13:21, "The Lord went before them [the Israelites] by day in a pillar of cloud to lead the way…" (NKJV).

Later in Exodus 24:15-17, a cloud covered the mountain and "…the glory of the Lord settled on Mount Sinai" (NIV). In Second Chronicles 5:13-14, when Solomon's Temple was being dedicated, "…the house of the Lord, was filled with a cloud…for the glory of the Lord filled the house of God" (NKJV).

This same glory cloud dwelled within the walls of the Azusa Street mission and even hovered around the outside of the building during the revival, every day and night for three-and-a-half years. On certain nights, flames could be seen shooting from the rooftop of the mission converging with flames shooting from the sky into the mission. This, too, is the Shekinah Glory described in Exodus 13 as the "pillar of fire" that led the Israelites by night. Also, in Exodus 24:17, "…the glory of the Lord appeared at the summit [of Mount Sinai] like a consuming fire."

Jewish teachers also believe the flames of fire are angels called *seraphim*, meaning "burning ones." The flames over Azusa were fiery angels coming and going from heaven, bringing miracles and returning to heaven to receive more miracles.

In John 1:51, Jesus said, "I tell you the truth, you will all see heaven open and the angels of God going up and down on the Son of Man, the one who is the stairway between heaven and earth." What a beautiful picture our Lord paints of Himself—the heavenly highway between earth and paradise. It is no wonder that when the "burning roof" lit up the night over Azusa Street, creative healing phenomena intensified, such as limbs growing out, all in the Name of Jesus of Nazareth.

This Shekinah Glory of God and these angels of fire are the heart of the Father visibly expressing "on earth, as it is in heaven" (Matt. 6:10), or as Pastor Bill Johnson puts it, "when heaven invades earth."

The Azusa Street Revival as experienced through the eyes of the children and the youth is what makes this book different from the rest. It is not a doctrinal or historical perspective. It is the up-close and personal experiences of the young people who were there. No one knew how the daily services were conducted before these stories were told. These youngsters even played hide-and-seek in the Shekinah Glory cloud as it filled the atmosphere.

This compilation of personal encounters reveals the heartbeat of the revival. These young ones delighted in the Lord, and He gave them the desires of their hearts (see Ps. 37:4).

The revival, which lasted for three-and-a-half years, the same length of time as Jesus' ministry, shaped the rest of their lives. Almost sixty years later, the youth of Azusa recounted this precious, privileged time to a young man named Tommy Welchel, who would listen to their stories and store them away in his mind and heart until God allowed them to be captured in print.

Woven into the beloved, original stories are new stories from Azusa Street, giving first-time readers a seamless revelation of this mighty move of God, while familiar readers discover anew the heart of the Father poured out at Azusa. There are also fresh, engaging details on the saints threaded into their accounts.

Continuing the journey that began at Azusa, this book reveals how God used these willing vessels, including Tommy, throughout their lives.

You will see how the saints continued to heal the sick and even raise the dead at Pisgah, a community where they lived in their retirement years. Tommy also will reveal the miracles that God performed through him while he lived with the saints at Pisgah during the 1960s.

Heaven is invading earth again, today. Tommy witnesses miracles of all kinds when he simply retells these blessed stories of a century ago. The hundred-year prophecy is, indeed, underway.

The saints of the Azusa Street Revival had only one cited sadness—the loss of the glory. Their common hope was to have it return in their lifetimes. These are their stories, as told to one young man who sat at their feet and listened closely.

WORD OF MOUTH: ORAL TRADITIONS

As a culture reliant on the written word, we can be skeptical about stories handed down by word of mouth. The stories in this book were told to Tommy Welchel, a storyteller himself. To dispel any doubt about the accuracy of the stories, it is important to understand this credible and legitimate form of communication called oral tradition—a tradition that is woven into the fabric of many ancient cultures.

The Israelites practiced oral tradition. The *Shema* is the central prayer in the Jewish prayer book. This ancient prayer is found in Deuteronomy 6:4 and begins, in Hebrew, *Shema Yisrael...* "Hear, O Israel! The LORD is our God, the LORD is one!" (NASB). It is a command to *hear*.

Our Bible is derived from oral tradition, both Old and New Testaments. The ability to read and write was reserved for the wealthy, educated few. The majority of people learned by listening and memorizing. Entire books of the Old Testament would be memorized by the Jews simply by listening to them being read by the teachers. Oral tradition, or storytelling, is a beautifully personal and intimate means by which to learn, as you picture young people gathered around their teachers or the elders of their families.

The Native American culture also practices oral tradition. Tommy Welchel is more than one-quarter Cherokee Indian from both his mother and father. The Cherokees recognize people within the tribe called "Keepers." The Keepers have been handed down the history of the tribe by sitting and listening to the tribal elders. Tommy is a "Keeper" from both sides of his family.

As a youngster in Chickasha, Oklahoma, Tommy would drink his RC Cola and eat his banana Moonpie while sitting and listening to the old men on the porch of the general store tell stories that dated back to before Oklahoma was a state in the Union. Tommy's inherited, cultural trait made him a natural to sit at the feet of the Azusa Street saints a decade later and listen to their stories.

God had it all planned out.

A God Thing

Yes, God had planned even my part in this amazing journey.

In the summer of 2008, a young, radiant Bethel School of Supernatural Ministry student named Melissa Cordell, who had no idea I was a writer, prophesied to me that she saw books stacked around me on a table. Across the table from me was God, and those books were the product of our conversations. That word has been pinned up on my wall and held in my heart ever since. Little did I know that God would sit across from me in the form of Tommy Welchel in the summer of 2012.

How I met Tommy can only be labeled a "God thing." I really don't want to overuse that term, but if you are like me, you're having more and more of those divine encounters that just can't be called anything else.

In February of 2009, Randy Clark and Global Awakening held a healing conference at the church my husband and I attended at the time. We were brand-new to a Spirit-filled church, which was the result of my reading Bill Johnson's book, *When Heaven Invades Earth*. Having been raised Catholic and then attending Methodist, Nazarene, and Calvary Chapel churches, Bill's book changed my faith and thus my life.

My husband, Marc, joined me on this awakened faith journey, and we embarked on a God adventure. We were on fire for all that we were discovering about God and found a church in September of 2008 that would feed our newfound hunger. By the time of the Randy Clark conference, we were enthusiastic about being vessels for the power of God.

Marc is really the one God used to bring about my meeting Tommy. On a short break between sessions one day of the conference, Marc perused the book tables on the way back from the men's room. He picked up a book with flames on the cover that mentioned something about Azusa Street. To us at the time, Azusa Street was a main thoroughfare in an old neighborhood in the San Gabriel Valley of

Southern California. We had no idea about the revival and William Seymour or the others. Marc thumbed through the pages quickly, spotting a couple of photos, one being a black-and-white portrait photograph of both William and Jennie Seymour. He didn't know who they were and neither did he have time to find out because the next session was starting.

Hours later, Randy invited everyone to the front who wanted impartation. Marc and I, gluttons for God, eagerly made our way to the stage. While we were waiting for impartation, Marc suddenly started laughing. The laughter then spread to me and everyone around us. We didn't know what it was called, but later found out it is termed *holy laughter*.

If you're unfamiliar with this term, it is a touch from the Holy Spirit, just like tears, peace, electricity, or the weight of glory. It is laughter that comes through you but from outside of you.

Later Marc told me that the face of a black man flashed in his mind when the laughter started. It was the man pictured in the book with the flames on the cover (William Seymour), but the mental picture was a close-up, not the full-length photo as in the book. It was a unique experience.

Through a series of events orchestrated as only the Holy Spirit can do, the man who was the storyteller behind the book with the flames on the cover, Tommy Welchel, was introduced to us at a gathering at our house. It was April 15, 2009. That date always represented Tax Day to me. That year, I playfully redefined it as Tommy Day.

Tommy and I stayed in touch over the next three years. When it came time for the new book, it seemed like a natural fit. Tommy gave me a great gift when he told me it felt right in his spirit to work with me. I've been writing for years in many venues—in broadcast and theatrical advertising, in freelance journalism...and my first feature script is underway.

So I assumed position as in the prophetic vision, and Tommy and I sat across the table from one another.

This book begins the stack.

INTRODUCTION

⌒∾⌒

"Train up a child in the way he should go, and when he is old he will not depart from it." (Proverbs 22:6 NKJV)

My Part in God's Plan

Mama couldn't read or write. She was completely illiterate. But when I was in her belly, she received the Holy Ghost. That's when God told her about me. Mama would drag me to all the great revivals, the tent revivals. I'm talking about Branham, Cole, Allen, and Roberts. From a little bitty kid, Mama would take me to them. I didn't know what was going on; as far as I was concerned, she just wanted to punish me.

I asked her why she didn't take any of my other ten brothers and sisters. She said "Tommy, the Holy Ghost told me you was going to be a preacher-man someday." Someday. She took me to all these meetings because she wanted me to come under these men's anointing and receive impartation from them. I, on the other hand, called the Holy Ghost a "rat fink" because He would always tell Mama when I was up to no good.

When I saw Branham in 1950, I was only seven years old. I saw that halo thing on top of his head when he was in Houston. It looked like it was breathing! I was glad I was sitting way in the back. It scared the tullies out of me. I crawled under the pew and hugged the iron legs. That was one man I didn't want to get close to.

By the time I was fourteen, I stopped going to revivals. I knew about the Gospel, but I didn't want it at that time. We lost our farm, and that event exploded my world. I was used to the river and the ponds and the trees, to the horses, cows, pigs and chickens. We moved to the "big city" of Chickasha, Oklahoma, which had a population of 14,000. All I could take was my dog. That triggered my rebellious period.

I was sleeping in bar ditches, haylofts and vacant houses. I started stealing to eat. You better not leave your clothes out on the clothesline overnight. If you did, they became mine. If I could wear them, I did. If I couldn't, they went in the trash bin.

I was no longer afraid of Mama. In the past, if I got mean, she would say, "All right, I'll talk to your daddy." Well, I didn't want Daddy to talk to me because he had a razor strap that would cut the blood right out of me, and he would use it. That man was mean. But by fourteen, my daddy went to the state prison in McAllister—the revenuers caught him selling corn liquor.

By the time I was seventeen, I had been living on the streets for fourteen months and was a criminal wanted by the police for burglary. Society was pretty much fed up with my lawlessness and was ready to lock me up and, if possible, throw away the key. The police wanted me and were looking for me big time.

An old friend of mine, Glen, came by and said, "Tommy, the police know who's been breaking in all those houses. The cops said, 'We want Welchel! We're gonna get him off the streets.' In fact, they have a warrant for your arrest, and they are gonna come by and get you."

꠷

Tommy would run from the law, straight into the arms of God. God's unlikely accomplices in His plan were two con artists—a guy named Teddy and Teddy's grandmother.

꠷

Teddy and his grandma were from Venice Beach, and they wanted to go back 'cause things were tough in Oklahoma. They invited me to go with them 'cause I had a reputation as a good thief. I could be sitting there talking to you and leave with the stuff from your pockets in mine.

I didn't really want to go to California and leave Oklahoma, but Glen reminded me that it was either go to California or go to jail. I went to Grandma and Teddy and asked if the offer was still open. They said, "Yeah." I told them that I had two big boxes of loot that we needed to go and get early in the morning—stuff I'd stolen. The next morning, we got my stuff and went on the run.

When we got to Venice Beach, Teddy and I got into a fight over a girl. I whipped Teddy, but I didn't get the girl. Grandma said, "Look, I like you, Tommy, but you can't stay here with you and Teddy fighting like this. You hurt him pretty bad!" So I got kicked out. I lost my place to stay *and* the girl.

꠷

Penniless, homeless and hungry, Tommy was another stray on the Venice Beach strand. He had an Uncle Ed in Bakersfield, but he didn't have any idea where Bakersfield was or how to reach him. As he sat there wondering what to do and letting the California sand sift through his toes, he had no idea how his life was going to change in a matter of minutes.

꠷

Well, I'm sitting there with this long face, feeling sorry for myself, not knowing where to go or what to do when I saw these two old ladies walking down the boardwalk. I was sure they were looking for someone to witness to. They had those "glory buns" that sat on top of their heads. The higher the bun, the more glorious you were. I'd seen them in all those revival meetings my mother took me to. I can recall that when those women would get to shaking by a touch of the Holy Ghost, the pound of bobby pins holding up those glory buns would start flying like machine gun fire! "Get under a pew!" I'd say. I had to take cover!

These two ladies came over and sat down, one on each side of me, and started talking to me. Now, I'm hungry and in my con mode, so I decide to play along with them, hoping they'll give me money or something to eat. One of the ladies was the landlady at the apartment where Grandma and Teddy lived. The other lady, kind of small and dainty, was called Sister Goldie.

Sister Goldie did most of the talking while the landlady sat there and held my hand. That felt good; she reminded me of both of my grandmas. They were talking about the Lord, and Sister Goldie asked if I knew anything about Him. I said, "Yeah." When they asked me if I wanted to pray the sinner's prayer, I thought to myself, "Man, you're here; you don't know anybody. What else are you gonna do?"

I said the prayer for these ladies because it was time to eat, and all 6'2" of me was hungry. At first I really wasn't serious. But as soon as I said the prayer, it felt like someone turned on an oven inside of me. I began to cry!

I looked at them in astonishment. Somehow these two women broke through a wall in me that had been built up for years. Preaching to me never worked. I'd rebel, and you didn't want to get me mad. I was liable to hurt you. I told them that I was now a Christian. Sister Goldie replied, "Well, I know you are, son."

Even though I began the prayer insincerely, God heard it. That day, that prayer changed me completely.

❧

The love and kindness of these two women touched Tommy deeply. Learning he had nowhere to go, they brought Tommy back to the land-lady's apartment where he spent the night on the couch. The next day,

Sister Goldie and Tommy took a long bus ride to Pisgah, a community where Sister Goldie had many friends and visited once a month.

Little did Tommy know that Sister Goldie, among others he was about to meet, had been at the Azusa Street Revival. He had heard about it in those tent meetings his mother took him to as a child. All those meetings of his childhood were in preparation for the next six years of his life. Tommy would live at Pisgah among the "Azusa Street saints," as they were affectionately called, from 1960 to 1966. He not only lived in their midst, but he also listened to them as they told him their stories.

Every month for that span of six years, Tommy would alternate visiting them and sitting at their feet as a sign of respect. Finding out he loved chocolate chip cookies and cold milk, they would serve him these treats while they recounted treasured tales from Azusa Street.

⌒∽◡⌒

I'm there at Pisgah about a month when Sister Laura Langtroff said, "Brother Tommy, you need the Baptism of the Holy Ghost."

"You mean that tongue stuff?" I knew what it was. My mother had done it all the time. She said yes. I didn't know if I wanted it or not.

She said, "Would you do me a favor if you're man enough?"

"What do you want?"

"Read the ninth chapter of Revelation and see if you want any of this to happen to you," she said.

Well, I read it. It scared me—things stinging me, giant things like giant scorpions, rocks falling on me but not killing me. The only people unbothered were the ones who had the name of God on their foreheads. So I asked Laura, "How do I get the name of God on my forehead?"

She said, "You've got it up there as soon as you start speaking in tongues."

I started wanting that tongue stuff. I wanted God's name on my forehead. The next night, Dennis Bennett's first wife, Jean Stone, John and Joan Baker and Brother (Pastor) and Sister Smith were teaching old-time Pentecostal songs. These people were what we called Charismatics—Episcopalians, Presbyterians, Lutherans, Catholics—who had received the Baptism but were staying in their churches. So Baker asked me if I would like to receive the Baptism. I said, "You mean that tongue stuff?" He said yes. I said, "Yeah!" Well, I got it. I was really happy.

A month after my Baptism, these Azusa Street people started coming around to me and saying, "Brother Tommy, we feel led of the Lord that you're the one."

I looked at Sister Carney. "The one what?"

"The one we're to tell our stories to."

I said, "I am a storyteller. I'm what you call a Keeper amongst the Cherokees. We keep the family history and can tell you what happened and when. I love stories."

They said, "Our stories are about Azusa Street."

"Oh, Brother Seymour?"

They said, "You know about him?"

I said, "Yeah, Mama talked about him." Some of the healing evangelists would talk about the great Azusa Street Revival where miracles happened.

I wasn't but seventeen when I first started sitting and listening to these old Azusa Street saints. I heard their stories over and over, every month for years until they died or until I left. I went to their apartments or wherever they were. Most of them lived on the grounds of Pisgah, but a few lived elsewhere. I never grew tired of sitting with each person—sometimes up to a few hours—so I could hear these great saints share their memories of this incredible move of God and His use of these willing and faithful young ones at Azusa Street.

I didn't know how many people were wanting these saints to tell them their stories—Demos Shakarian, Tommy Hicks, David du Plessis—but they wouldn't tell them. They said, "God will bring the one we're to tell our stories to." It was me. I kept the stories right here in my head where they have been for more than forty years.

THE PROPHECIES ARE COMING TO PASS

The Hundred-Year Prophecy

⊷

Sometime in 1910, Seymour just stood up on the stage, took the box off his head and started prophesying. He said in about a hundred years there would be another revival like Azusa Street. Only this time it would not be in one place. It would be all over the world. There would be a return of the Shekinah Glory and the miracles. This revival would not be with just one person or just pastors. It would be with everybody in the Body. This time the revival will not end until the Lord returns.

Seymour repeated this revelation more than once. All the saints told Tommy this prophecy.

On the opposite coast in New York City, according to Charles Parham's granddaughter, Parham just stood up one day and declared the same prophecy, using almost the exact words. This happened within a couple of days of Seymour's prophecy. They both pronounced that this modern-day outpouring would surpass Acts 2, Topeka, and Azusa.

Celebrate! We are now in the hundred-year period, and you are alive in this time!

According to Jesus in Luke 10:24, we are the envy of prophets and kings to see such an outpouring of the Spirit: "For I tell you that many prophets and kings wanted to see what you see but did not see it, and to hear what you hear but did not hear it" (NIV).

The hundred-year prophecy is coming to pass as you will see in chapter 18 called "Modern-Day Manna: Miracles of Today." The telling of these stories has triggered this next mighty move of God and fulfilled prophecies spoken over Tommy decades ago.

⊷

William M. Branham's Prophecy over Tommy in 1960

I was at Clifton's Cafeteria in downtown Los Angeles for a Full Gospel Businessmen's meeting of about a couple of hundred people shortly after I received the Baptism of the Holy Spirit. Branham was the guest speaker this day. He walked by and I said, "Praise the Lord, Brother Branham!" I wanted him to look at me. I wanted Branham to see me this time. I was no longer afraid of him. I had the same Holy Spirit he did. He stopped, looked at me and then went on.

He took about one step, then wheeled around, laughed and pointed his finger at me, and said, "You're the one."

I said, "Yeah."

Later on, I thought, "Wait a minute. The one what?" I didn't know what he was talking about. This happened on a Saturday. By Monday, the saints started to tell me their stories.

Tommy Hicks' Prophecy over Tommy in 1961

I met Tommy Hicks, an Assembly of God preacher, and all of 5'3". Prior to 1950, he didn't even know where Argentina was on the map. However, he's the one whom God called to Argentina in 1950 and had the great revival in that country. Tommy Hicks is the one who converted Juan Peron, the president of Argentina. It is now an Assembly of God nation.

I met him while I was living at Pisgah. We went walking one day near the Rose Bowl, and he told me about the vision he'd been having over and over and over. This mountain, which was the church, started melting down, and a river started flowing from it, and every now and then a giant would get up and walk out of it. He said, "Call them giants or generals. I call them giants."

I said, "Okay."

Finally he said, "Tommy, a lot of years from now, you will be one of those giants." I got embarrassed. I'm nineteen then, but I still got embarrassed. I'm a simple country boy from Oklahoma.

I said, "Oh…that'll be you and Shakarian and Smith and Branham and Roberts and…."

"You stop," he said. "Now, you take this seriously. Brother Tommy, listen to me. We won't be here, but you will be."

I didn't realize what he was talking about would happen forty years later.

Jean Darnell's Prophecy to Tommy in 1966, the Sixtieth Anniversary of Azusa Street

Jean Darnell took over the pastorship at Angeles Temple after Aimee Semple McPherson. One day she came to the Herald of Hope office at Pisgah where I worked. She said, "Brother Tommy, I have a word from the Lord for you.

"The Lord is showing me that all these stories that the Azusa Street saints have been telling you, and you have been learning and memorizing, will someday be put into a book."

I thanked her for her kind words, thought about what she had said and then hid her words in my heart. I'm not one who goes and starts trying to make God's prophecies come to pass. If it's prophesied to me, I just never forget it; I never do forget, but I let God take care of it.

"Be Patient and Be Obedient"

Now, I've seen Jesus twice. The last time I was visited by Him, I was in my favorite hiding place, up in the attic of the church in 1963. I had hiding places all over Pisgah when I needed to be by myself. The only light was my flashlight. I wanted a visitation, and David du Plessis told me to simply started whispering, "Jesus."

I thought I had whispered it only five or six times, but the alarm that I had set for two hours went off. I turned it off and then froze. It was like daylight in there. I looked down at my flashlight and it wasn't on. It wouldn't have made that much light anyhow...and I thought, "The light, the light. Jesus!"

I looked over and saw the most beautiful sandals.... I've never heard anyone say they saw Him in sandals before. He wore these beautiful, jeweled sandals, and a robe I can't quite describe. It was snow white, but you could see little strands of gold and some little, tiny jewels—the most beautiful piece I ever saw.

I looked up, and it was Jesus. I leaped and grabbed Him with a bear hug around the waist and put my head in His stomach. I wasn't going let go of my Lord!

I felt His hand stroke the back of my head, and He said, "Tommy… be patient and be obedient." He kept repeating, "Be patient and be obedient," over and over and over.

I kept listening because He kept stroking the back of my head, and I enjoyed that. All of a sudden, it was daylight outside. I think He just talked me to sleep because that was the only way He was going to get away. I was not gonna let go.

I thought, "What was this experience all about?" Later on, I'd want to tell one of these stories of the saints to somebody. I'd start to, and I'd hear His words, "Tommy, be patient and be obedient."

I couldn't tell any of the stories until the year 2006 (one hundred years after the start of the Azusa Street Revival). And then, all of a sudden, it was like a fire in me. I just had to tell! That was the first book.

I met a woman associated with Billye Brim's ministry. Her name is Lynn Kellog, and she was a young starlet in Hollywood who did a couple of Elvis movies. She now lives up on Prayer Mountain and sings nothing but patriotic and gospel songs.

One day she came walking by, and I said, "Hi, Lynn. How are you doing?" She stopped, looked at me and started crying. I said, "Lynn, what's wrong?"

She said, "Brother Tommy, I feel like you didn't tell all the stories."
I said, "You're right."

She let me know that I wasn't getting any younger and I needed to start telling the rest of them.

I guess God agreed. I didn't die when I should have in 2010. I've got more stories to tell in this second book.

1

CODE 4

My wife wanted me to get a checkup for my high blood pressure, and I was grossly overweight. I weighed well over 300 pounds, but I wouldn't listen.

On Friday evening in September of 2010, I wasn't feeling very well. I didn't feel well through the weekend, so I made plans to go see Dr. Brown on Monday. By Monday, my left arm was hurting. I headed over to Dr. Brown's, but he had closed that office and moved to Integris Hospital, which was only about two miles away.

I got back in my car and drove out onto Mustang Road. There was a sign to a clinic—"Mercy After Hours." I was feeling so poorly that I didn't even try to get to Dr. Brown's place. I pulled in, got out and staggered into the clinic. I sat down and looked at an orderly and said, "Young man, young man, please."

He says, "Yes, sir."

"I need a doctor or a nurse or something. Please." He went and got a nurse, and I could see a nurse looking at me through a haze. Then I passed out.

I came to and an ambulance was there and the fire department. "Mr. Welchel, you're having three heart attacks right now."

I asked, "Can you do that?"

"Yes," the fireman said.

I said, "Well, hey, guys, can I just drive myself to the hospital?"

"Sir, you just shut up and stay where you are. You're not in charge here. We are. Sir, you're having multiple heart attacks. If we don't get you to the hospital in a hurry, you're going to die."

I said, "Oh, dear." I heard the fireman on the microphone, yelling, "Code Four! Shut down all entrances to I-40 and to I-44 to Baptist Hospital. We've got to be there within five minutes or this man is gone." Again, I thought, "Oh dear."

I pulled my phone out and dialed my wife. She said, "Hello?"

"Marlene? Listen, do you hear the ambulance? I'm on my way to the hospital."

"What's wrong?"

"I'm having a heart attack," I told her.

Marlene called Billye Brim and told her what was happening, and Billye told her, "No! I need Tommy. The church needs Tommy! He's just like the one crying in the wilderness. He's the one to bring us the encouragement, the stories to wake us up and to realize this is what it's going to take. Marlene, we're going to go into prayer. We're not going let Tommy go!"

Marlene said that Billye prayed for about twenty minutes. She said she could feel the anointing coming over the phone. About a dozen people were praying at Prayer Mountain.

I reached Mike at Billye's hotline. They all recognized my voice, and I said, "Mike?"

He says, "Hi, Brother Tommy, how are you doing?"

"Listen, I need prayer. I'm having a heart attack. I'm on my way to the hospital. If God doesn't intervene, I'm going home. So let's see what God will do. I want His will done."

Mike said, "Tommy, I turned you onto a loudspeaker. Everybody's praying. Some of them are standing on top of their desks praying."

I said, "Thank you. I need that."

I hung up and lost consciousness for two weeks. I don't remember getting to the hospital. I don't remember my daughter talking to me. I don't remember my wife getting there a few days later. I don't remember anything. I was out.

When I came to, the doctor told me what had happened, showing me a little chart. "The two arteries going into your heart shut down, and the two arteries going out of your heart shut down. No blood was coming in or going out. We've never seen anyone survive this kind of heart attack and bypass surgery."

I asked, "Why am I alive?" That's when the doc looked down, then looked back at me teary-eyed.

"Mr. Welchel, we don't know. It was a miracle."

Truth is, I'd rather be in heaven than here. I've visited heaven three times, which I'll describe later in this book. But I'm lying there in that hospital, and I thought, "I haven't gotten all the stories out, have I, God?"

I do have more stories to tell. People will ask me why I didn't tell all the stories the first time. I only tell what the Holy Spirit leads me to tell at the time.

I've been called the "last living link to Azusa Street." I guess that means that I have to live. To tell more stories. To encourage God's people....

2

THE GENESIS OF AZUSA STREET

Say Hello to Sister Carney and Brother Seymour

⤳

Azusa Ages: 17 and 36

The police officers politely forewarned, "Either shut it down or rent a place like a regular church or auditorium. You have gotten too big to continue to meet at this home." The home was on Bonnie Brae Street. The man the police cautioned was William Seymour.

The revival meetings held there began as small gatherings led by William Seymour. They now flowed out to the front yard, the neighbors' yards and onto the street as Brother Seymour preached from the porch of this small home in the Los Angeles area.

Not only was Bonnie Brae filled to overflowing, but the power of God also was reaching one block away to Beverly Boulevard. Innocent people, walking across the street, would fall out in the Spirit, speaking in tongues, not even knowing what was happening to them. It was 1906, so a turn-of-the-century traffic jam ensued since the horses pulling the buggies wouldn't step over the people lying in the road.

Seymour had been invited to move from Houston to pastor a church in Los Angeles. He preached his first sermon on the Holy Spirit one Sunday morning and returned that night to preach again. The door was padlocked, and a note informed him that he was fired. They didn't want this strange stuff.

Mr. Asbury was a member of this church. He came up to Seymour and said, "I knew they were going to do this, but I've got a house over on Bonnie Brae Street. You can preach from there." The Asburys also happened to be one of Frank Bartleman's prayer groups, praying for revival.

Brother Seymour realized that he needed a much larger gathering place as the crowd grew larger and larger with each passing day. Looking for a place to meet, he found an abandoned warehouse that at one time was used as a Methodist church. The warehouse was perfect, and the only thing keeping Seymour from renting the building was money.

That night, the need to move was heavy on Seymour's heart. He prayed to God for direction and before the evening was over, he had received his answer. God instructed him to get on a trolley car as soon as the service ended and go to Pasadena. There was one hitch. By obeying God's instructions, Seymour was going to break the law—the sundown law—which stated that no person of color could be on the streets of Pasadena after dark.

True to God's leadership, Seymour didn't argue but trusted and obeyed. He rode the trolley until God instructed him to get off, then followed as God guided him to an apartment nearby.

Sister Carney, just a teenager but married, had arrived in Pasadena earlier that day. She was to meet with several of her friends who had been members of the First Baptist Church. They were hungry for the Baptism of the Holy Spirit, which somehow didn't fit Baptist doctrine. They had been meeting together for months now in the apartment of one of the members of this group. This particular evening, they were coming together to pray for revival. They were certain that God was about to do something big in the Los Angeles area.

Around 10:30 p.m. and after hours of fervent prayer, God brought together two elements of a force that would usher in one of the greatest manifestations of God ever experienced by man since the birth of Christ.

Seymour walked up to this apartment where God had led him and knocked on the door. Startled, the ladies went to the door together and opened it. They found a black man, blind in one eye, standing before them. Instead of slamming the door and calling the police, which would have been reasonable given the day and age, the owner of the apartment apprehensively asked, "Can I help you?"

The answer to this simple, fretful question would startle and astonish those gathered for prayer. After several months of fervent prayer, God responded in an unusual manner.

Seymour replied, "You're praying for revival, right?" When the ladies responded with a unanimous yes, Seymour made a bold statement: "I'm the man God has sent to preach that revival."

Without hesitation, the ladies invited Seymour in. The prayer meeting that evening and those present were not coincidental. God had been preparing many for the miracle of Azusa. Without this ordained meeting, Azusa may have never happened. After some excited chatter, he preached to them and took up an offering that was more than enough to rent the Azusa Street warehouse.

At this point, it is really important to understand Sister Carney's role in realizing the revival at Azusa Street.

At the turn of the last century, many girls were married at the age of fourteen after they completed eighth grade, which was considered high school at that time. Sister Carney was one of these young brides. In a prearranged marriage, she married a man of nineteen after he completed college and had a job. This was 1903.

In 1904, at the age of fifteen, while attending church services at Pisgah, which you will read about later, Sister Carney responded to Dr. Yoakum's teaching on the infilling of the Holy Spirit evidenced by speaking in tongues. She was one of the first to receive the Baptism.

Her love for the Lord and her desire to introduce others to the exciting experience of being filled with the Holy Spirit led her to Pasadena. There she witnessed to several of her friends who were members of the First Baptist Church. By 1906, these ladies had been asked to leave the Baptist

Church because of their beliefs. Unbeknownst to them, God was setting the stage for a miraculous work of the Holy Spirit.

❧

When I met Sister Carney in the early 1960s, she was in her mid-seventies, standing about 5'9" with a slender build of about 130 pounds. She was a typical little old granny, with a gray-haired glory bun sitting on top of her head. She walked slowly with short steps, always wearing a pleasant smile. She had an older face with a little pointed chin, and when she smiled, her lips kind of sunk in. She still wore those flowery dresses ladies wore at the turn of the century. And yes, she wore granny boots—those little boots with little hooks and eyes.

About every third Monday night, I would walk to Sister Carney's apartment. As I approached her home, I would smell the enticing aroma of fresh-baked chocolate chip cookies waiting for me. Once a month on a Monday, I had the privilege of sitting at Sister Carney's feet on a small throw rug in front of her wooden rocker. While eating cookies and drinking a cold glass of milk, I listened to her tell her Azusa stories like the one that begins this chapter.

Sister Carney was one of my favorite storytellers because she could tell the stories of Azusa in better detail than anyone. Everybody appreciated this about her. Although she normally had a little high-pitched voice, when she told her stories, her voice was soothing, yet filled with an excitement that had lasted for more than sixty years.

Sister Carney was seventeen years old at the start of the Azusa Street Revival. In fact, she was there from raising the rent for the building, to the first day they entered to clean the building, until they padlocked the door. In the beginning, even with the money Seymour raised for the rent from Sister Carney and her friends, the old, dingy white warehouse still needed a lot of physical labor to get it ready for use. She and her friends from the apartment joined the group from Bonnie Brae to prepare the dirty, cluttered building to serve as a worship center. They removed all sorts of junk that had accumulated through the years. The warehouse had even been used as a barn, housing all sorts of animals. Isn't it interesting that God chose yet another humble dwelling to house His Presence over 2,000 years later?

Sister Carney recalls that Brother Seymour assigned each of the volunteers an area to clean the mounds of animal waste. With a warm smile, she told how grateful she was for the task of cleaning up the area that housed the small goats with their small droppings rather than cleaning up after the horses and cattle.

After cleaning out the warehouse, the volunteers gathered and set up wooden fruit crates they had found thrown away behind the nearby grocery store. They placed two by twelve planks across the crates to serve as benches throughout the meeting room. With only meager funds but unlimited ingenuity, these volunteers labored side by side until the meeting place was ready to be used however God desired to use it. Thankfully, God had provided them a place large enough to house the anticipated services.

During one of our Monday night meetings, I asked Sister Carney, "What miracle do you remember that happened through you?" She smiled and her lips kind of sunk in as the excitement welled up inside her.

"It was the woman who caught her husband with another woman. She had gotten into a fight with her and the adulterous woman bit off her ear." Sister Carney was smiling, but I laughed out loud. She gently chided me for laughing and said, "Brother Tommy, it's not funny to catch your husband with another woman and then for the two of them get to fighting so badly that the other woman bites the wife's ear off!"

Here's the story as I recall. When the wife entered the meeting room, she was holding a bloody bandage to the side of her head. Sister Carney noticed she appeared to be in tremendous pain and went over to minister to her. While waiting for Seymour to come down and the meeting to begin, Sister Carney asked her what had happened, and the lady told her about the fight. She told her that she didn't have the ear with her, and Sister Carney reached over and pulled the bandage off to see the wound that basically looked like a bloody, raw piece of meat.

Without hesitation, she began to pray for the woman. After praying for her, the lady said that the pain was gone. Sister Carney looked at her wound again, and to her astonishment, right before her very eyes, a brand-new ear began to grow out. Sister Carney sat there with her mouth open and simply exclaimed, "Oh my God!"

This wasn't the first miracle that Sister Carney witnessed, but it was the first one she witnessed as a result of God working through her own prayers. As she told me this story, she recalled it as if the miracle had just happened the night before.

I asked Sister Carney about other miracles she witnessed or participated in. With a smile and a twinkle in her eyes, she talked about the mighty works of God. According to Sister Carney, many people in wheelchairs and cots were brought in from the hospitals around the area. Often, before Seymour would come downstairs or even when he was sitting with the box on his head, Sister Carney and others would go to the sick and crippled and pray for them, and they would get their healing. For those in wheelchairs, she and others would pull up the footrests, pray for them, and then watch them walk off, pushing away the empty evidence of their prior handicap.

Sister Carney remembered a man who shook with Parkinson's disease so badly that he was wheelchair bound. She walked up and just looked at him. His family said, "Aren't you going to pray for him?"

She answered, "When I'm ready." Truth is, she said, he was shaking so badly that she was looking for the chance to grab his head.

She recalled that he was quite an attractive man in his mid-thirties. Finally she took his head in her hands, but not before she had put up the flaps of his wheelchair. This became known as the Carney Rule— the flaps of a wheelchair must be up before praying to show faith! She grabbed hold of his head and took authority over the disease, commanding it to be gone in Jesus' Name.

The man started calming down. Pretty soon he was out of the chair and up dancing around! I asked her, "Did you dance with him?"

She said, "I was a married woman."

"I don't mean that," I said. "Were you dancing, too?"

"Yes, but not with him."

I just smiled at her.

One of these wheelchair healings stayed with Sister Carney in a special way. One man had heavy braces on his legs and had not walked in years. She recalled that his wheelchair had wheels made of wood. She prayed for him, and he was miraculously healed. His name was Brother Aubrey, and he was pastor of a big church in Los Angeles. I actually got to meet him because he would come to Pisgah to see his precious Sister Carney.

During one visit to Pisgah in the 1960s, Brother Aubrey shared his version of the healing miracle. Sister Carney didn't say a word to him. She just walked up, pulled the footrests up, put his foot down, then got the other foot, lifted it up and then laid it down. Remember his legs had very heavy braces on them.

Next, she told him to get up and walk, but Aubrey told her he couldn't walk because of the heavy braces. Sister Carney responded by getting the people who were with him to take off his braces so he could walk. They did, and he did! He got up and walked.

I was amazed at the story and asked Sister Carney about how many miracles God had used her to personally perform. She told me that God blessed her by using her two to three times a day the three to four days she attended each week. That's six to eight miracles a week for over three-and-a-half years. Do the math!

Our talks turned from miracles performed by God through the faithful saints to the difference in miracles when Brother Seymour was preaching. Sister Carney explained that when Brother Seymour would come down, there were even greater miracles. Seymour never had a set pattern; rather, he would come down and put the box over his head. Then he would take the box off when directed by God, get up and do what God told him to do.

Sometimes he would go to a certain section of wheelchairs or to a certain section of cots for people who had been carried in from the hospital. She explained that, to her astonishment, Seymour would point at them and say, "Everyone on the cots or wheelchairs, you're healed in the Name of Jesus." Everyone on the cots or in wheelchairs would get up and walk around fully healed of whatever malady he or she suffered.

Our conversation would turn from the miracles performed by Seymour to Seymour himself. He was blind in one eye and the son of slaves. He listened and learned about the Holy Spirit from Charles Parham who preached in a suburb of Houston called Pasadena, in Texas.

Seymour sat outside the sanctuary and listened through a crack in the door. He couldn't go in and sit with the congregation because of his color and the Jim Crow laws. But Seymour didn't get mad. He just sat outside and listened. He wanted whatever they had, and he got it.

In a short time, Parham would be sending people like John G. Lake and F.F. Bosworth to Azusa Street to come under Seymour's anointing before they went into the mission field. "Before you go overseas as missionaries, go to Azusa Street. Make sure you become friends with Seymour. Make sure you hang around him," Parham instructed. "Get all of his anointing that you can."

God loves irony—the black man who had to sit outside Parham's doors became the man whom everyone sought. The world came to Azusa.

The segregation that Seymour and so many sadly experienced stands in great contrast to what Azusa Street became in that same period of history. Azusa Street was the first fully integrated church in America. Seymour almost became fanatical about it. When he would come down from his apartment above the church, if twenty or more of the same color were sitting together, he'd split them up. He wouldn't tolerate it. He said we were to be one in the Lord.

He went as far as saying that once a person becomes a Christian, he or she becomes a new creature that never existed before and belongs to a different race—the Christian race. We stay the same color, but we are all one race. In fact, when the saints told me their stories, they never mentioned the color of the person they healed. Ever. It's as if everyone was "color blind." Frank Bartleman said it simply: "The color line was broken by the blood."

It was in Houston at Parham's church that Seymour met Lucy Farrow, who nannied Parham's children. However, Parham had Lucy around to do more than just watch his young ones. She carried such an anointing that whomever she touched would immediately start speaking in tongues.

Lucy was the one who brought Seymour to Los Angeles. Eventually, she would become the first missionary to be sent out from Azusa Street. I wanted to know more about Seymour, this great man with whom I was awestruck.

Mama Cotton was also another missionary who came from Azusa Street. She would establish more than sixty churches in the Los Angeles area. Mama Cotton blew a shofar, and when she did, the Shekinah Glory would fall. Aimee Semple McPherson invited her to Angelus Temple to speak, and when Mama came, she brought her shofar.

She'd preach for about thirty to forty-five minutes, then she'd say, "It's time for God to go to work." She'd blow her shofar, and the Shekinah Glory would fall. Great miracles followed. Seymour wanted everyone who was at Azusa Street to go out and spread what was there into their neighborhoods, cities and the world.

Sister Carney, a treasure chest of information, was happy to oblige. Her story continued with the box on his head.

When Seymour came down to the meeting, he would sit down and put a box on his head. At first it startled Sister Carney. Sometimes he would sit with the box over his head for ten minutes and sometimes it would be an hour or more. Although the practice seemed ridiculous,

Sister Carney realized that he was obeying God, no matter how silly or ridiculous it appeared.

That apparent act of humble obedience led to mighty power when he removed the box. This act of humility was critical to the power God displayed through Brother Seymour.

Seymour and Sister Carney became friends, and after Seymour married, Sister Carney would often join them for dinner. Even in a social setting, she would feel the anointing on Seymour. She recalled that Seymour was very pleasant to be around. He was a humble man who always had a gleam in his eye, a smile on his face and a deep, resonating voice.

There was no question about his anointing of God. She recalled that if you touched Seymour, a kind of electricity would shock you. The current was so strong that the first time she touched him during a meeting, she almost passed out. Even his wife, Jennie Moore, would often have to move to the couch from their bed because she couldn't touch him during the night without feeling the electricity.

When Brother Smith, our pastor at Pisgah, asked Sister Carney what caused the miracles at Azusa to stop, she replied, "It stopped when Brother Seymour stopped putting that box over his head. When he quit coming down and putting the box on his head, it started dying."

Sister Carney said that she asked Seymour why he stopped, but he wouldn't answer her. Over the years, he suffered increasing ridicule and persecution because of the box, especially as his reputation grew as thousands upon thousands came to Azusa over the three-and-a-half-year period.

My co-author, Michelle, had a compelling, maybe controversial, thought. She said, "Seymour always listened and obeyed God. That's why he put the box on his head in the first place. Why would he suddenly stop? If he saw the Glory withdrawing, why would he not put that box back on his head as quickly as he could? "Fear of man, possibly. But what if God told him not to put the box on his head any longer? The Glory was there for three and-a-half years, the same length of time as Jesus' ministry. Perhaps God intended it to last only that long." Michelle continued, "Remember, many, such as John G. Lake, came to Azusa for the anointing, received it, and then went out into the mission field, encouraged by Seymour to take Azusa Street to the world. Revivals end, but the anointing remains with those who seek and receive it.

"Maybe Seymour never answered Sister Carney's question because it would only raise more questions—questions whose answers belonged only to God." Michelle concluded, "Seymour might have been *obeying* God by never putting the box back on his head. We will never know."

It's true. We can only surmise now. However, Michelle's point makes me remember a conversation I had with a professor of Church History at Rhema Bible Training College in Broken Arrow, OK. Surprisingly, this professor told me that his own research revealed that most of the big revivals lasted only…three and a half years.

I asked Sister Carney how old Seymour was when he died and what he died of. She said that he was only fifty-two years old in 1922—not old at all. She sadly recalled that many people turned on him, and the ultimate offense happened in 1913, three years after the Shekinah Glory ended.

At the Arroyo Seco Revival of 1913, no one knew him or acknowledged him. He felt a failure. Though no one really could say what Seymour died of, "I think he died of a broken heart," Sister Carney offered.

I have a book titled *The 100 Most Important Events in Christianity*. Seymour and Azusa Street are listed and remembered in that book. His heart may have been broken, but he was neither a failure nor forgotten. He is in eternal glory now.

Of course, any discussion about Azusa turned to the Shekinah Glory. When I asked about her experience with the Presence of God's Spirit, Sister Carney's face would light up. She described it as being a part of heaven. To her, it was like breathing pure oxygen, and to her wonderment, it was always present.

When I asked her to describe the flaming Shekinah Glory reported by many, she told her story. She remembered the fire department coming because of a call that the building was on fire. When they arrived, they didn't smell any smoke or see any evidence of fire. She didn't run out with the firemen. She recalled that it was Seymour, Bosworth, Lake, Smith, and Sines who ran out.

Lake explained that the fire was coming down from heaven into the building, and fire was going up from the building and meeting the fire coming down. Fascinated, Sister Carney went out one night, walked about a half a block and saw the awesome sight for herself. To her, this divine connection of fire coming down from heaven and going up to heaven was just further evidence of God's mighty Presence in that place.

Sister Carney noted that although the Shekinah Glory cloud, the "misty stuff," was present all the time within the building, this divine, fiery connection wasn't an everyday occurrence. Whenever this connection was present, the power of God was even more intense within the meeting and the miracles even more amazing.

I wanted to know how the services were conducted every day. Sister Carney could usually answer all my questions. Seymour came down in the morning, the afternoon, and again in the evening. He'd stay about three or four hours each time. He had an apartment right above the "sanctuary," where he'd pray for seven hours a day, eat and sleep.

There were people coming and going all the time, even late at night. We're talking about hundreds a day throughout the twenty-four hours. If somebody wanted to get up and say something, they could. No one interrupted Seymour when he was at the meeting, but anyone could get up and talk. Seymour didn't care, except you couldn't get up and be out of line.

As we talked, she would mention some of the other young people at Azusa. She was not the only young person running around being used of God to perform His miracles. She teamed up with C.W. Ward and Ralph Riggs, two young men who would later become instrumental in helping to found The Assemblies of God Church, the largest Pentecostal movement in the United States and the world.

She would invite them to go with her as new people arrived and see if they could minister to them. These young men, who were around thirteen or fourteen years old, partnered with Sister Carney and went throughout the crowd, wanting to be used by God to perform miracles and help people get healed. These were teens running around having a ball, praying over people and looking for people who needed healing.

Sister Carney was also very close to John G. Lake, who had received the Baptism of the Holy Spirit up in Zion, Illinois, and came to Azusa as a young man as instructed by Parham. He later became a great missionary and was used mightily in South Africa as well as in the United States.

Lake stated that at Azusa Street, God told him that any disease that came in contact with him would die. While he was in South Africa during an outbreak of Bubonic plague, he insisted that some of the "live" disease be put on his hand. They took a sampling after it was in contact with him and looked at it under a microscope. "My God, it's dying!" Within seconds, the sampling was dead.

Some have credited Lake with stopping the Bubonic plague in that region. Back in the States, in Spokane, Washington, Lake opened up healing rooms and closed down hospitals. (Though the original building where Lake housed his healing rooms burned down in a fire years ago, the Spokane Healing Rooms were re-opened on the same location in 1999 and are still in operation.)

Sister Carney is what I would call an Azusa legacy. Her undimmed excitement and enthusiasm as she re-lived these stories with me each month allowed me to experience Azusa through her eyes. Like John the Apostle, she shared with me what she had heard, had touched with her hands, had seen with her own eyes and experienced in her own heart from the beginning.

3

A JOYFUL NOISE

Say Hello to Brother Sines and Brother Christopher

∼≈∼

Azusa Ages: 26 and 18

Sister Carney and Brother Sines were the best of friends and spent many hours in the gardens at Pisgah talking and re-living Azusa memories. He endearingly recalled Sister Carney as the ringleader of it all, directing the goings-on in the warehouse.

Naturally their conversations would turn to Seymour and how he was unpredictable. Once he took the box off his head, God surely would move mightily through him. But how? Who? Who would be healed? How would it happen? Would fire light up the sky again?

One thing was certain—there would be music. Seymour would stand up and instruct the people to sing a certain song. Hundreds of voices blended their way up to heaven. Seymour would sit and sing with them, his eyes closed as if the music itself were a holy offering to God.

Soon after the singing started, Seymour would say, "Sing in the Spirit!" Whenever that happened, heaven itself came down and filled the room. The music was beyond description—pure, powerful, sanctified.

These melodies became known as a "new song" as the crowd began to sing in a heavenly language, sometimes in tongues, sometimes without words. At times, it seemed as if angels joined in the singing of these new songs led by the Spirit of God.

Although singing in the Spirit was already a part of many of the services, when Brother Sines and Brother Christopher became part of the leadership team, the music reached deeper into heaven. With the addition of piano and violin, the new heavenly song went beyond the ordinary to the extraordinary.

Brother Sines was about twenty-six years old when he came to the Azusa Revival in about 1907. He was a bit older but still quite young to be a part of the leadership team that led the services.

I met Sines at Pisgah in 1960. I stayed in a three-story men's dormitory where Sines was Dormitory Director for all the single men staying at Pisgah. He stood about 5'9" tall, and was heavyset but not obese. When I met him, he walked stooped over a little bit but didn't use a cane. I can still see his receding hairline—about one-third of it gray—his dark eyes and a good-sized nose.

Like the others, I would go to Brother Sines' room about once a month. I would sit at his feet, and while munching on chocolate chip cookies and drinking some cold milk, listen to his stories about Azusa. He had a mild, pleasant voice and spoke softly.

Unlike the others, I had a deal with Sines that I would come and clean his apartment if he would tell me his stories. True to my word, I would first mop his floors with a dry mop and then with a wet mop. The floors were covered with linoleum so they were easy to clean. When I was finished, we would sit down and Sines would tell his stories.

A concert pianist who later worked with a well-known band leader named Tommy Dorsey, Brother Sines was all about music and fondly recalled his role in the music at Azusa. Seymour would lift the box from his head and often ask Sines to begin singing a certain hymn or song. At first, Sines would begin the song and lead the crowd in singing the request of Seymour.

Later on, Sines brought his own piano to the meeting place. Then when he was instructed to sing, he would begin playing the song on his piano and leading the music. Without sheet music or a hymnal, whatever song Seymour wanted, Sines would sing and play the song from memory. He told me, "Tommy, I'd sit and watch my fingers move, and it sounded like a thousand pianos playing." The other saints also said that, many times, it sounded like a thousand pianos playing. It makes me think of Revelation 5:11: "I heard the voice of many angels around the throne…ten thousand times ten thousand, and thousands of thousands (NKJV).

Sines recalled with joy the experience of singing in the Spirit. He remembered that virtually every time Seymour instructed them to "sing in the Spirit," something wonderful and beyond understanding would happen. The music would rise to a new level, and the sound that came from Azusa was like a heavenly choir singing.

I asked Brother Sines about the miracles at Azusa and if he personally was ever involved in them. He would smile and, in his soft voice, begin to share with me his first and favorite miracle.

Seymour had not yet come down to the meeting. Sines was on the platform leading the crowd in songs when he saw a young crippled boy on crutches sitting off to the side, unnoticed by those going about the crowd performing miracles.

Sines came down from the platform, approached the young boy and asked him why no one was ministering to him. The little boy shrugged his shoulders with a kind of "I don't know" shrug and said, "I'm just waiting for someone to come over and pray for me."

Sines asked the child, "Do you believe that God is going to heal you?"

The boy, with a look of anticipation on his face, said, "Why, yes!"

Sines took the crutches from him, laid them down on the floor and then laid hands on the boy and prayed for him. At first nothing happened, but then the boy began to exclaim, "I feel it, I feel it!" He leaped to his feet, dancing, running and shouting with Sines right behind him.

The next miracle that Brother Sines described to me actually came looking for him. An old gentleman, who could hardly walk, hobbled up to him one day while he was still playing the piano. He called him by his first name.

"Charles," he said. Brother Sines looked up. "I have crippling arthritis." The man showed him his hands. They were swollen and gnarled.

Brother Sines talked with the man and found out he had played the piano for a star-studded church in Hollywood called Hollywood Presbyterian Church. Of the 7,000 members, there were celebrities of the day such as Dale Evans and Roy Rogers. He couldn't play anymore because of this condition. "I want to play the piano again," he said.

Brother Sines got up and told the man, "Sit down there," pointing at the piano bench. The man sat down, and Sines laid hands on him and prayed, "In Jesus' Name, play." He looked at the man's hands, still swollen. He said again, "Play!"

The man started to play as best he could. As he played, his hands began to shrink as the swelling disappeared. He kept playing!

I never got to meet the man because he was older at the time of Azusa. Brother Sines told me that he returned to Hollywood Presbyterian and got his old job back as well as his life.

Like many others, Sines was drawn to the power and anointing God had given Brother Seymour. Unlike others, Sines was on the platform with Seymour, and at least fifty percent of the time, he was able to sit right next to him.

Brother Sines was obsessed with "the box." The reason he would try to sit next to Seymour whenever possible was to get close enough to the box to see and hear what was going on inside. It did not matter if the box was on Seymour's head ten minutes or one hour. During that time, Sines could not pay attention to anything else, observing the box and Seymour the entire time. He would sit there thinking,

"God, are You talking to this man, or is he just sitting there waiting, listening or meditating?"

When Sines was out eating or fellowshipping with Seymour, he would ask him about what was going on in the box. Seymour told him that he was meditating, waiting on God. Seymour noted that when he would speak to God, he could hear himself talk, but it was always a whisper, and always in tongues. Sines asked Seymour if he understood what he was saying in tongues, and Seymour responded yes, he knew.

Sines recalled that there was a glow around the box while it was on Seymour's head. He observed the glow but told me he dared not touch Seymour or the box. He was afraid of what would happen. He would lean over as close to the box as possible and just listen, but he would never get close enough to accidentally come in contact with the glow or the box.

He recalled one of the miracles he observed that was performed through Seymour while the flames were shooting out of and in through the roof of the warehouse. The whole place was full of the Shekinah Glory.

This miracle involved a man who had smoked a cigar all his life. He always had one stuck in the corner of his mouth. The mouth grew cancerous where the cigar touched. Brother Sines said that it was eaten away, and there was a hole in his cheek. What wasn't eaten away was black and rotten. Brother Seymour said, "It's gotten some of your teeth, too. How long does the doctor say you got to live?"

The man could hardly talk and said, "No more than a year."

Seymour answered, "Now, they're right, but God can change it." The man said yes.

Seymour slapped hands on him, began to pray and then took his hand away. The black was gone, and they watched missing gums, teeth and flesh fill in where there were none before! Can you imagine that?

Brother Sines observed many things from the platform, and he commented on young Ward's style and his silly facial expressions.

Sines recalled that Ward was comical to watch, but that God worked through him in a mighty way.

He also commented that Brother Anderson must have been kin to the kangaroos the way he bounced around. He would watch Anderson get so excited that he would climb on a bench to see everything. When great miracles happened, he said that many times Brother Anderson would go berserk and wind up somewhere in the church, not knowing how he got there. Just moved by the Spirit, I guess.

Brother Christopher, a young man around eighteen years old, joined Brother Sines about six months after Sines came to Azusa. Christopher owned a Stradivarius violin and would bring it to Azusa to accompany Sines when he played the piano.

I met Christopher while I was at Pisgah and actually lived with him in the dorm. I found him to be one of the politest men I'd ever known. He was a very small, frail man, weighing around 110 pounds, and standing about 5'5" tall. He was also one of the most trusting men I'd known.

We lived with about twenty guys in the dormitory, and always about five or six of them were not saved because they had been taken off the streets. Now, Brother Christopher would simply slide his Stradivarius under his bed. Those men could easily have sold that priceless instrument for ten dollars on the street. So Brother Smith made him turn it in to him for safekeeping when Brother Christopher wasn't practicing.

By the time I met him, he was in his seventies but still had a full head of coal-black hair. He was somewhat dark skinned and told us he was part Italian. Extremely shy and quiet, Brother Christopher didn't just talk; you had to pull words out of him.

He and Sines were great friends and played many concerts together in the years following Azusa. In fact, Sines and Christopher went to Great Britain to play a command performance for a very distinguished woman named Victoria of the House of Windsor. Queen Victoria sang some of the songs they played. She gave them very high honors and instructed them not to give the glory to themselves but to God.

Like Sines, Christopher loved the music at Azusa and confirmed that the experience of singing in the Spirit was unequalled by anything he had ever experienced in his musical career. An accomplished concert violinist equaled by few, he would share with me that when he played in the Spirit, he played at a level he'd never achieved even in his greatest concert. He, too, said that he would just watch his hands moving while hearing thousands of violins.

Brother Christopher also talked about the Shekinah Glory and told me that he even tried to bottle it. To his disappointment, there was nothing in the bottle the next day.

Brother Christopher was an observer. Because of his shyness, he didn't go out into the crowd. People seeking healing came up to him while he was on the platform. Christopher remarked that people must have thought he was someone important because he sat on the platform.

I asked Brother Christopher, "Did anything happen to the people you prayed for?"

He would quietly say with a smile, "Oh, yes, Brother Tommy. Oh, yes."

He fondly told me about praying for a blind man whose wife had brought him to Azusa. The wife led her husband by his right hand while he held his white cane with the red tip in his other hand. She brought the man up to Christopher and said, "My husband is blind. Heal him."

Christopher quietly said, "I can't heal him, but I can pray for him, and Jesus will heal him."

She said somewhat demandingly, "Okay, do it!" Brother Christopher humbly and obediently prayed for the man. He was instantly healed.

I asked, "Didn't that excite you and make you want to do more?"

Christopher replied, "Why, yes, I wished more would have come to me."

Brother Christopher told of a young man who had burned his arm at work. The arm was badly infected and green with gangrene. It was so bad that Brother Christopher said that his arm should have been amputated.

Christopher prayed for him and told him to go home and clean the wound and then bandage it. The man went home, cleaned and bandaged the burn, and came back the next night completely healed.

Christopher was impressed with the man's willingness to be obedient to God's guidance and do what he was instructed to do. The following evening when the healed man returned, Brother Christopher rejoiced with him as they celebrated the awesome miracle from God.

One night parents of a teenage boy were half carrying him up to Brother Christopher. The boy had suffered a brain hemorrhage. I don't know if it was from an accident or what, but he had been this way for four or five years.

Pitifully, they asked Brother Christopher, "Will God heal him?"

"Yes!" Brother Christopher answered and then asked, "Do I have your permission?" He was a sweet, little guy. The parents said yes, and he said, "Bring him to me."

He started talking to this teen, and the parents told him that the boy didn't know what he was saying. Surprisingly firm, Brother Christopher said, "Leave me alone. Do you want him healed? Then leave me alone."

He explained he was talking to the boy, but he also wanted the devil to hear what he had to say. "I don't care what anyone says. You're going to be delivered." That's how they talked at Azusa—completely confident in God.

Brother Christopher said he got all bubbly and happy. "You're going to be normal…and you're going to be used of God. Satan did this to you, but Satan is a liar. He's really nothing."

Brother Christopher kept preaching because he wanted the devil to take note. Finally he said, "Now, I'm going to lay hands on you and take authority over this, and you are going to be delivered."

Brother Christopher reached out and put his hands on the boy's head, pushed tightly and began to rebuke the damage the devil had done. He rebuked the hemorrhage and commanded all blood clots, everything, to clear up. He demanded, "Not tomorrow. I want it done now in Jesus' Name!"

The boy jerked and fell down off the platform onto the ground, kicking and jerking. Brother Christopher stood at the edge of the platform and looked at the parents, who were upset. "If you're in fear, go away," he told them. They said that they were okay. He assured them, "Just don't worry."

Finally, the boy stopped jerking and kicking, and Brother Christopher commanded, "Now, get up." The boy looked up at him and started trying to get up. He didn't remember how.

"Help him and walk him because the child doesn't know how to walk. He'll learn quickly, just help him." Within ten minutes, the boy was running, leaping, jumping, worshipping and praising God. Forever changed, the boy went into the ministry when he became an adult.

Christopher only performed a few miracles because of his shyness, say four or five a week compared to that many every day like Carney, Sines, Garcia, Anderson, and Dundee. However, they were mighty works of God and bore witness that if you were at Azusa and your heart was right, God found a way to involve you in His miraculous works. If something like shyness kept you from going to the people, God in His marvelous ways would bring the people to you.

Many times while at Pisgah, I had the privilege of hearing Brother Sines play the piano and Brother Christopher play his violin. Sometimes my mind would meander to the days of Azusa. I would sit at Pisgah wondering what it must have been like to hear them play when God's Spirit took the music to a heavenly realm as the people sang a new song. I remember someone writing or saying that the music was like the very breath of God coming forth from human vocal cords. I could only imagine.

4

AS ZEALOUS AS ZACCHAEUS

Say Hello to Brother Anderson

AZUSA AGE: 15

Just as at the house at Bonnie Brae, so the crowds at the Azusa Street warehouse had grown from a handful of faithful followers to hundreds now gathering several times a day to witness and experience the miracles of Azusa and the anointing of Brother Seymour.

Among those attending was a fifteen-year-old named Brother Anderson, who attended the Azusa Street Revival faithfully. He was one of the first to receive the Baptism of the Holy Spirit at Azusa and be a part of this mighty work of God. Although he was just a few inches under six feet tall, when the crowd gathered, Brother Anderson often found it difficult to see what was happening throughout the building as miracles were being performed by many of his teenage friends.

The sight of Brother Anderson climbing on top of the benches was not uncommon. Like Zacchaeus of old, who climbed into a sycamore tree to get a better view of Jesus, Anderson wanted a better vantage point to witness the marvels and moves of God.

I met Brother Anderson at Pisgah where we became great friends. Whenever I would see him, whether at church or at his home, Brother Anderson would see me coming a block away and would come bouncing down the street saying, "Well, Brother Tommy! I'm so glad to see you." And I was always glad to see him!

Brother Anderson had a medium build and shiny eyes that glowed. His slicked back, gray, balding hair accented his ruddy complexion. You could recognize him from afar because of the bounce in his walk. Remember Brother Sines jokingly considered him kin to a kangaroo. I could see why.

Perhaps his most memorable characteristic was that he always had a beautiful smile on his face and was always bubbly and happy. In all the years I knew him, never once did I see him frown.

I had the privilege of going to Brother Anderson's home about once a month on Thursday evenings. I would be at least a block away when he would come out to meet me halfway with a spring in his step and welcome me to his home. Unlike the ladies, Brother Anderson didn't have homemade cookies, but he'd have cold milk and store-bought cookies waiting for me.

I still remember the way he would dress. He would have on a plain, long-sleeved shirt buttoned all the way up, including the top button, and always tucked in. He wore slippers and regular slacks with a belt rather than suspenders. Out of respect, I would sit at his feet on a barren wooden floor as he settled into his vinyl-covered rocking chair. Perhaps "settled in" is not quite the way to describe this adventure. He didn't really sit in his chair; he would sit on the edge of it. When he began to tell his stories, he would throw his hands up, bounce in his chair and excitedly explain different miracles he had seen or prayed for at Azusa. As with all the saints, the sheer delight of what happened at Azusa was never dulled by the passing decades.

The image of Brother Anderson and his home lives in my memory. Here is this old man, living in a sparsely decorated apartment, with few furnishings. One picture hanging on the wall that stood out was of John G. Lake and Brother Anderson side by side in a picture taken about sixty years earlier. Although his possessions were few, this man was rich in priceless memories and invaluable experiences that gold could never buy.

It was a sweet ritual: "Tell me again about your days at Azusa," I would say to start the discussion. Brother Anderson would excitedly come to the edge of his chair and, as he began his stories, you could feel his characteristic bounce in his words.

Often his own personal experience was his starting point. Although he was born again before attending Azusa, there he received the gift of speaking in tongues shortly after the revival began. He recalled that when he spoke in tongues, he would do so in a loud voice, as if someone had turned up his volume.

As soon as he blared out "tongues," to his amazement and shock, someone interpreted what he was saying. When recalling the entire experience, he would describe it as being in heaven. He longed to see another revival like Azusa.

From tongues to healings was a logical progression. Brother Anderson told me that many who were blind and deaf were healed and that he was a part of many of those healings. Some were older people, some were middle age and some were young—teenagers just like him. If he wasn't part of the miracle happening, he was most likely standing on a bench watching other miracles take place.

He told me that he had attended Azusa only about ten times when God first used him in helping people receive healing. A young man, not much older than Brother Anderson, had a clubfoot, and when he entered the meeting, he tried to hide his disfigurement. He explained to Brother Anderson that he didn't want people feeling sorry for him.

Brother Anderson asked the young man, "Are you aware of the Shekinah Glory? You don't have to have this." He went on to explain to the young man that Jesus, when He died on Calvary, received thirty-nine stripes on His back, and those stripes were for this young man's healing.

The young man replied, "But that was for sickness and disease; I just have my foot turned sideways."

Brother Anderson replied, "God will heal it! You should see some of the miracles here."

The young man finally believed a miracle was possible, and Brother Anderson began to pray for him. To their astonishment, shortly after the prayer, the foot didn't just pop out, but rather it just started to slowly move outward. In a matter of minutes, the young man was jumping, running and shouting. The foot had been deformed since he was a young child and had just gotten worse the older he grew. Yet, in just a few minutes, the foot was healed and perfectly formed.

Brother Anderson was right behind this young man dancing and shouting also. This may have been the first time God used Brother Anderson to work a miraculous healing through faith and prayer, but it was far from the last.

Brother Anderson recalled praying for a woman much older than he was with a big knot just above her wrist. She didn't know what it was, but it hurt. When he asked her about the pain, she told him that she couldn't even work at home. Rather than lifting, she would scoot things with her arm. Brother Anderson told her that she didn't have to do that because Jesus would heal her.

He reached out, barely touched the knot and said, "In the Name of Jesus, be healed." In seconds, the knot was gone. Immediately she got so excited that she started doing a dance right there on the spot, and Brother Anderson became her dance partner.

I was captivated by his stories. I asked him about the greatest or most unusual healing or miracle he had witnessed, and he told of a miracle that left me full of wonder.

A younger woman named Diane, maybe in her late teens or early twenties, with two young children, walked into the revival meeting with her hand supporting a large growth or tumor about half the size of a basketball on the side of her head. She looked pitiful.

Before she could even get seated, people, including Brother Anderson, started surrounding her. Anderson told the woman that

God was going to work a miracle for her. She kind of rolled her head and her eyes but didn't say a word. She came to get a miracle, and all she could do was nod her head yes.

As the people began to lay hands on her, the tumor or growth began to shrink. The woman was speechless. She stood there gasping and finally yelled, "I'm healed!"

Through the grace of God, I got to meet Sister Diane while I was at Pisgah in the 1960s. She wasn't obese, but she wasn't a little woman. She stood just under six feet tall with a broad face and a marvelous spirit. I asked her about the healing, and here was what she shared with me.

She had heard that things like miracles were happening at the Azusa Street warehouse. She even saw the flames going up and coming down. So she thought to herself, "What have I got to lose? I'm dying, and if I go there and I die, so what! The doctors can't do anything. They can't operate because it is too big to cut off." She said, "So I waddled myself down to Azusa, holding my growth in my hands."

A little embarrassed, she walked into the meeting. Shortly after the miracle happened, she remembered Brother Anderson being right in the middle of the miracle and just fell in love with him.

That miracle not only saved her life but also propelled her into a ministry that would impact thousands of people over the years. With just twenty-five cents to her name, she started a soup kitchen when she was in her early twenties and was still serving soup to the needy and downtrodden almost sixty years later when I met her.

Of course, I always wanted to know more about Brother Seymour, and Brother Anderson, too, was more than willing to oblige. He loved when Brother Seymour would come down to the service. Young Anderson would sit near him and try to peek under the box to see if Seymour was praying at all. He would lean as far down as possible to try to see, but he could never peer under the box.

Seymour would sometimes sit for ten minutes and sometimes for over an hour, doing nothing but sitting with the box over his head. Anderson would spend the same amount of time fascinated by the box and watching Brother Seymour to see even if his hands or feet moved. Much like a statue, Seymour sat perfectly still most of the time he was under the box.

Brother Anderson was in awe of Brother Seymour. He told me that Seymour was one of the sweetest men he had ever met. Tradition tells us that when Seymour got married to Jennie Moore, two women got upset because they felt he didn't have time for marriage with the return of Christ so imminent. These ladies got so upset that they stole his mailing list and ran off to Portland. That incident really upset young Anderson.

Anderson was so inspired by Seymour that he tried to imitate him. A few times he would get up and say with youthful enthusiasm, "Everybody in this section that needs healing, stand up and be healed." Anderson learned very quickly that the anointing God had bestowed upon Seymour could not be duplicated except as God willed. Anderson would go back to laying hands on those needing miracles.

Young Anderson believed that Seymour was a man of faith who never doubted anything. Every time he opened his mouth and said something, it happened. I learned from Brother Anderson that Seymour was a brilliant preacher. Seymour would come out with phrases so intelligent and profound yet simple enough that the most uneducated could understand him. The wisdom of this man was phenomenal.

The greatest thing that impressed Anderson was when the Spirit would fall on Seymour and he would start working the gifts. Anderson would get up on the benches so he could see Seymour talking to the people. Quite a few times Seymour would point to maybe a dozen or so people with what looked like rheumatoid arthritis and say, "You want to see a miracle over there? Every one of you within a few minutes is going to be up and walking in the Name of Jesus." And every one of them—you could hear their bones popping—would be up shouting as their legs and arms and hands straightened out.

A few times Anderson witnessed Seymour perform one-on-one healings. One such healing stood out in Anderson's memory. A man whose face was deformed with small growths all over it came to Brother Seymour. The deformed man looked very homely and ugly. Brother Seymour prayed for him, and immediately the growths began to fall off his face, restoring his face and making him whole. Volunteers had to come and clean up those growths that had fallen from the man's face to the floor.

As long as Seymour was there, young Anderson didn't shout or dance. His eyes were totally fixed on Seymour. Anderson confirmed that this power stayed with Seymour until the time he stopped placing the box over his head.

After talking about Seymour, the transition to the Shekinah Glory was logical. I asked Brother Anderson to describe what the Shekinah Glory was like, and he again brightened up as he came to the edge of his rocker.

Anderson told me that the Shekinah Glory was hard to explain because it could only be described, but not understood. At times he would come into the building and there would be a kind of glow. There were times when God would start moving and working, and a smoke-like substance would begin to glow even brighter.

People could walk through it, and sometimes it would sort of roll. You couldn't take a fan and blow it out, nor was it something you could pick up. Brother Anderson confessed that he tried because it looked so tangible. He remembered that at times the mist would get so thick that it would fill the whole building. Even Seymour was fascinated with the heavy mist that filled the room. In fact, there were times that Seymour would take his feet and kind of play with the thick cloud.

Brother Anderson was awed by the Glory and described it as a part of heaven coming down. You could walk in it, sit down in it, run your hands through it and breathe it into your lungs, but you could not capture it.

I pressed Brother Anderson to tell me about the "fire." He said it looked like flames about fifty feet in the air coming down into and going up out of the roof to meet and merge in the sky over the warehouse. Young Anderson would just stand there with his mouth open. He didn't know how to explain it, but it was real. He told me the burning bush described by Moses finally made sense.

Like the other saints, Anderson noted that whenever the people worshipped by singing in tongues, the power was greater and the anointing fell on the service.

One of the favorite traditional songs sung by the saints gathered at Pisgah was intricately linked with their encounter with God's Glory. The song that they sang with great enthusiasm was appropriately entitled, "Heaven Came Down and Glory Filled My Soul."

Before the stories ended, I wanted to know about the other teenagers Anderson hung around with at Azusa. Much like Sister Carney, Anderson remembered both Ralph Riggs and C.W. Ward being a part of the group of young people who went around praying for people to be healed and being used by God to perform His miracles.

Anderson recalled a story about Ward that he thought was somewhat comical. Ward had a unique way of praying for somebody. He would swing his hips and go through all sorts of dramatic gestures. It was almost a theatrical production. He would do these big, long prayers, swing his shoulders and hips and yell out, "In the Name of Jesus!"

I asked Brother Anderson if God used Ward to bless others. Anderson would smile and say, "Well, they did get healed!" Ward was young just like the rest of them and was going through his teenage years. Although his actions may not have been conventional, those years at Azusa prepared both Ward and Riggs to be powerful vessels for God in the future.

As I mentioned earlier, young Anderson also became good friends with John G. Lake. One of Anderson's prized possessions was the picture of Lake and himself that still hung on his living room wall six decades after Azusa.

Brother Anderson's vivid recollection of his personal encounters with miracles and the Shekinah Glory made Azusa come alive for me once again. The timeless excitement of all these saints never faded but remained shiny and new and allowed me to capture the awe experienced during this unprecedented revival.

5

LIKE MOTHER, LIKE SON

Say Hello to Brother and Mother Riggs

⚬

AZUSA AGES: 12 AND 35

I had a unique opportunity in this next story. I not only was able to meet Ralph Riggs, who was only twelve when he came to Azusa Street, but I also came to know his mother as well—a double portion blessing.

I met "Mother" Riggs at Pisgah in 1960. I must confess that she made the best chocolate chip cookies, bar none, and she made them big and round.

Mother Riggs was in her mid-thirties when she was at Azusa. By the time I met her, she was in her nineties. She told me that she mainly watched "Ralphy"—a nickname that wasn't Ralph's favorite—run around and be used of God. Ralph and his best friend, C.W. Ward, didn't complain that they had to be at church. In fact, they preferred to be in church rather than anywhere else! Wouldn't that make any mother proud?

Mother Riggs wasn't just a spectator. She, too, was actively involved in healings and miracles and spent much of her time with Sister

Carney. Although she mainly participated with others, God also used her when she was by herself.

Mother Riggs had bright, beady eyes that would just glow as she started talking about Azusa, and they glowed even brighter as she told her stories. She told me of her experience with about a dozen elderly people who reminded her of her parents. They were all brought to the meeting in wheelchairs and didn't have any major deformities or diseases. They were just old and feeble.

She learned well from Sister Carney about expecting miracles, and if anybody in a wheelchair needed to be ministered to, she would put the footrests up before she prayed for the person. Immediately after the prayer, these frail, old people got up, hooked their arms together and began to dance. Mother Riggs was so thrilled to see old people up dancing and worshipping the Lord that she joined right in.

Mother Riggs told me that she also prayed for a man who couldn't put any weight on his ankle due to the pain. She asked him, "Did you come to be healed?"

He told her, "Well, everybody is getting healed here they tell me. They just come and get healed, and I want my ankle healed."

She laid hands on his head and prayed for him. Within moments, the ankle that had been twisted popped and was healed. He stood up and began to dance and shout, and Mother Riggs just marveled at the miracle.

Like all the others, Mother Riggs loved the Shekinah Glory. She told me that the main thing she missed was the power of the mist or cloud as it glowed. She was convinced that the Glory they experienced was a part of heaven, and she was walking in it, living in it and breathing it in. She was also convinced that the abundance of miracles happened because of the Shekinah Glory and the Presence of God in the meetings.

I loved her stories, and I loved the fact that she not only supported her son, but also was right there with him as he enjoyed being used by God.

On occasion Ralph Riggs would stop by Pisgah to visit with his mom. I met him when he was in his seventies after God had used him mightily to advance His Kingdom. During four of those visits, I had the honor of spending time with him. As mentioned earlier in this book, Ralph and C.W. Ward were instrumental in founding The Assemblies of God Church. Even though I knew he had stories in abundance about the Assemblies of God, I wanted to know about Azusa and his teenage years there.

Brother Riggs told me that he appreciated the fact that he wasn't just a spectator watching older people do miracles; God also used him. He was given the liberty to go to anyone and everyone he wanted to and pray for them, and to his astonishment, they all got healed.

He wasn't quite twelve at the time of Azusa. He experienced Azusa with his best friend, C.W. Ward, who was two years his senior. "Tommy, C.W. and I couldn't wait to get to church in the evenings. When most kids don't want to go, we couldn't wait to get to church and have this fun of getting people healed and delivered." Riggs noted that each of them had six or more miracles or healings every night.

I asked Brother Riggs about the kids he hung around with at Azusa. He told me that Sister Carney was his favorite. He commented, "You kind of did what she told you to do. No one appointed her to be in charge; she just was a natural leader." Riggs also told me he loved to talk to and play with Brother Anderson, and, of course, there was Brother Ward.

When I asked Brother Riggs about his most memorable miracles, he shared a few of his many, many experiences. He recalled one where this old woman came to the church in a wheelchair because some disease had paralyzed her from the waist down. Ralph was just shy of his thirteenth birthday, so he was still only twelve. He got all excited when he saw her. "Why were you excited?" I asked.

"She reminded me of my grandmother," he said.

The woman became a little testy with him because he was trying to pick up her feet to put up the flaps. "You don't understand the Carney Rule. We must put the flaps up before we pray for you because you're going to be healed. You're going to jump out of your wheelchair and run." She protested in disbelief.

"Now, listen to me," he said. "You have to stop griping and nagging and going on. We're going to pray for you, and you're going to be healed. Don't argue with us. This is Azusa Street. You see the glory here? You're going to be healed!" She didn't say anymore and sat there looking at him.

He prayed for her. He had to pray for her twice and pray hard. Finally, he reached down and laid hands on her backbone and her hip. All of a sudden, she popped. Little Ralph said, "Take off running!" She just looked at him. "I said take off running!" She jumped up and took off.

"What did you do?" I asked.

"Mama and I took off with her," he said. "But we couldn't outrun her." A twelve-year-old boy couldn't outrun a grandma. I just love that.

His most memorable miracle was this large, gawky guy, in his early twenties, who stood over 6'5" tall and weighed over 250 pounds. He came into the meeting with booze on his breath, slurring his words and reeking of stale alcohol.

Riggs felt a voice inside of him saying, "Pray for him." Brother Riggs went over to the man and realized that not only had he been drinking, but he was also blind. Somewhat stunned, Riggs looked at him and said, "You can't see, can you?"

The man said, "No, that's what I came here for." Riggs, now somewhat more compassionate, prayed for him, and he was instantly healed. Not only were his eyes healed, even the stench of liquor was gone.

The man just sat for a while crying and sobbing and finally said, "Well, it's true. It's true. I'm healed." Here was a homeless, blind alcoholic restored through the miraculous power of God.

Later in life, this man was used of God to preach revivals and establish many Pentecostal and Assemblies of God churches across the midwestern United States. Riggs noted that he had the privilege of visiting many of these churches in his travels with the Assemblies of God. As a matter of fact, the First Assembly of Chickasha, Oklahoma, that I attended many times was started by this man, just a blind drunk on skid row.

Brother Riggs also told of his one and only mass healing. A group of people came from a retirement home and had minor problems like aching joints. Riggs decided he would try a "Seymour" and have a mass healing. He looked at them and said, "Every one of you are going to be healed in the Name of Jesus. Now, all of you, be healed!" Unlike every other time he tried to mimic Seymour and failed, this time Riggs witnessed a mass healing, as the joints cracked and were restored.

Although God used Brother Riggs in countless miracles, he chose to share only one last story. Two people, a husband and wife, came in wheelchairs, pushed by their teenage children. They were both very sick and had either pneumonia or really bad colds.

Brother Ralph went over to them and asked, "Did you come down here tonight believing God is actually going to heal you?" The husband said yes. Riggs began to pray for them but stopped suddenly as he remembered the "Carney Rule." He put up the footrests before finishing his prayer.

The stage was now set for God to work a miracle. Riggs got between the couple, placed his hands on their foreheads and prayed, commanding them to be healed in the Name of Jesus. They both had terrible fevers and the first thing Riggs noticed was that their temperatures went down. Within moments, the woman began to shake and, shortly, was up and running. The man just stood up, raised his hands and screamed in a very loud voice, "Thank You, God! Thank You, God!" God had healed them instantly.

Most of the time the Shekinah Glory was spoken of with reverence, but there was one time Brother Riggs revealed a lighter side. He told me that when Seymour would come down from his apartment, the Shekinah Glory would get so thick that you could hardly see the ground. With a sly smile, he confessed that when it was this thick, he and Ward would get in the back of the room and play hide-and-go-seek in the mist. My mind would wander back to his days at Azusa, and I could picture him running around full of life as he and the other youth were involved in this awesome outpouring of God.

Since they were just young teenagers at Azusa, I asked him if he ever tried to put Seymour's box on his head. He said with great respect, "Nobody touched Seymour's box even when he wasn't down there. It was sacred."

I asked him to seriously talk to me about the Shekinah Glory. Brother Riggs explained the experience much like his mother did. "I tasted a bit of heaven. Ward and I would talk and share that Azusa must have been what heaven is like. God must have sent some part of heaven down here."

One day when I was with Mother Riggs, she said, "Now, Tommy, tell my stories back to me." She had told me her stories four times. I said okay. I sat down and told them to her.

She said, "You've got them down perfectly. That's good."

I said, "Okay, but I don't want to quit coming."

"Well, tonight I'm going home," she answered.

"Back to Mississippi?"

"No, Tommy. I'm going *home.*" She was almost one hundred.

The next day, Brother Smith called me over to Mother Riggs' house. He said, "The sisters are telling me that Mother Riggs said she was going home last night. They said they even heard her telling you she was going home."

I said, "Yeah, what's going on?"

He said, "She's dead. Come in here. Look at her."

We walked into her bedroom. She was lying there with her arms folded and a big smile on her face. I looked at him and said, "She looks happy."

He said, "She went home." The Shekinah Glory she sorely missed was now hers forever to enjoy.

6

WHAT'S IN A NAME?

Say Hello to Sister Lucille and Sister Laura

❧

AZUSA AGES: 18 AND 16

Television star Lucille Ball wanted what Sister Lucille had—her last name. Sister Lucille's last name was McGillicuddy. Lucille Ball paid Sister Lucille handsomely to use it as the maiden name of her television character in *I Love Lucy*.

But her name is not all that she is remembered for. Sister Lucille McGillicuddy made quite a name for herself by becoming the secretary for Aimee Semple McPherson and her successor, Jean Darnall. Before that, she was one of the youth who impacted the lives of many during the Azusa Street Revival.

I met Sister Lucille at Pisgah. She couldn't have weighed much more than ninety pounds and stood under five feet tall. She was very slender and petite. Like many of the Pentecostal women of that day, she had long hair that almost touched the floor but wore it in a glory bun held together by a host of hairpins.

She was one of the Azusa saints whom I had the honor of listening to as I sat at her feet and munched on homemade chocolate chip cookies. Yes, I washed them down always with the cold glass of milk she had waiting for me.

During her Azusa days, she was part of the Carney-Riggs-Ward-Anderson group and was instrumental in helping many receive healing. I would begin our time together by asking her to tell me about the greatest healing or miracle in which she personally participated. She always told of two miracles that were a vivid part of her memory.

First she told me about the lady who had one leg shorter than the other. Her name was Goldie, and she had polio, causing one leg to be more than four inches shorter than the other. Sister Lucille insisted that Goldie take the brace off and allow God to heal her. Goldie told Lucille, "If I take the brace off, I better be healed."

Sister Lucille smiled and said, "You will be! Now take it off." She took off the brace, and Sister Lucille immediately prayed for her. As Goldie and Lucille sat there, the leg lengthened. Lucille told her to get up and walk. She took her first steps and almost fell over because she was not accustomed to walking with normal legs—miraculously both legs were the same length.

Next, with a twinkle in her eye, she would tell me about the woman whose wrist was shattered in a domestic squabble. The woman couldn't use her hand at all. Sister Lucille said, "It looks like your wrist has been crushed!"

She responded, "My husband hit it with a mallet. He was mad at me and thought he would teach me a lesson and crushed my wrist."

Sister Lucille told me that it just broke her heart. She earnestly wanted the lady healed and when she prayed, she all but begged God to heal her. After her prayer, she said to the wrist, "I say in the Name of Jesus, you do what I told you and be healed!" Immediately the lady's wrist was totally restored.

Sister Lucille's next story was not a cookies-and-milk story. It was more like a toss-your-cookies story. She would tell about the miracles performed on people who had very bad teeth, and usually I would lose my appetite. Lucille would have them open their mouths, and she would stick her fingers on the teeth that were bad and pray for healing. I asked her, "Were they infected and filled with bad stuff?" She would look at me with a half grin on her face. I said, "You stuck your finger on their teeth?"

With that half grin on her face, she said, "Yeah."

"What if there wasn't a tooth there?" I would ask playfully.

Sister Lucille took her story over the top. "I would stick my finger on the bare gum. In fact, many times I would push against the gum and let the new tooth push my finger up. On the really decayed teeth, all the bad stuff would come out, and we would use a handkerchief to rub the bad stuff off and there would be a new tooth. Even crooked teeth would straighten."

Usually teeth rotted because of diet and/or poor hygiene. This next story she told me was of a child whose second teeth grew in rotten and black from the start. The mother asked, "Will God heal this?"

Lucille said, "God will heal anything. And I love praying for teeth."

Lucille brought the girl over to her and asked others to get a handkerchief and a cup. Lucille took the handkerchief and laid it over the child's mouth. She prayed, and then a handful of blackened teeth just dropped out of the girl's mouth and into the cup.

Can you imagine what that this girl is thinking as this little woman is taking out her teeth? Completely toothless, the child just kept looking at her. Lucille told her, "Now, Jesus is going to give you a new set of teeth, and we're going to have fun getting them in there."

She went through the child's whole mouth, pressed on her gums, and teeth grew in one at a time. She could have had them all done at one time, but Lucille wanted to play. That little girl's teeth grew in perfectly. "Did it hurt when the rotten teeth were coming out?" I asked. Lucille said the child felt nothing. However, when the new, "Jesus teeth," came in, the little girl said, "It kinda tickled."

I just sat there shaking my head. Even though her descriptions of the teeth often caused my stomach to turn, I sat in awe at the miracles she described.

She would ask me, "Tommy, wouldn't you love to see those kind of healings in our services today?" I would just nod in agreement.

What impressed Sister Lucille was that the miracles were not confined to Brother Seymour. She would comment, "A little bitty woman like me could walk up and command a leg to grow out, and it would grow out. A busted wrist would grow back together. Rotten teeth would be replaced with brand-new teeth, and missing teeth would grow back in."

I asked her if she ever worked with someone who had all his teeth missing. She said "No, I never tried that."

I teasingly said, "Well, you should have."

She rebukingly replied, "I just never tried that, Brother Tommy."

I would meekly change the subject and ask her to describe what the Shekinah Glory was like. She would get such joy in her eyes as she told me how much she loved to be in the center of the mist-like cloud. She was so little in stature, she would sit down in it and, when it was thick, the mist was about up to her neck. Like a kid, she would have fun and play in the mist. She would often lie down, breathing it in. She could feel the energy of it and described that it was like pure oxygen being breathed into her lungs. She could smell it, too. The scent was like lilacs to her. Others said it smelled like roses. The aroma depended upon what part of the building you were in at the time.

When Brother Seymour was there and they would sing in the Spirit, Sister Lucille told me that the Shekinah Glory would just rise and fill the whole room, and you could breathe so much better.

Sister Lucille had a best friend, Laura Langtroff, who moved to Pisgah in 1955. Sister Laura became a part of Azusa when Lucille invited her to attend the revival.

When I met Sister Laura at Pisgah, she was in her seventies, stood about 5'7" tall, and weighed around 170 pounds. She and Sister Lucille looked like Mutt and Jeff when they were together because Lucille was so small. She had dark brown, very long hair and kept it up in a glory bun. Sister Laura came from a very well-to-do family and was a wealthy woman in her own right, but she chose to live at Pisgah with her Azusa friends.

When I would talk to Sister Laura, she would tell me about Azusa through her eyes. She and Lucille both worked with a lot of people who had trouble breathing. They loved ministering to women and especially to those who were old and feeble. Legend has it that if a woman came in with a cane or crutches and got near Sister Laura, she would be healed and walk away from the meeting free of any aids.

I remember asking Sister Laura, "How many miracles or healings did you participate in?"

She thought for a moment. "I attended every night, and there were at least three or four a night!"

She remembers a little boy, about nine or ten years old, who was demon possessed. His family kept him strapped down in a wheelchair because he was very violent and hard to control. "You'd better be careful, or he may bite you," his family told her. He'd hiss and foam at the mouth. He was just totally possessed.

Sister Laura got excited. She said, "This is going to be fun!" She started talking to the demon, until somebody finally rebuked her. "Laura, you need to do what you're supposed to do. Stop playing." So she reached quickly and grabbed the boy by the head.

She took authority over the demon. "Come out, in Jesus' Name!" The demon said it would come out, and it did. But the boy didn't get any better. "He has many demons," she realized. She smiled real big and said, "I'm talking to the next demon that's in charge." She spent about an hour casting out devils. Do you know how many demons that is?

I asked her, "How did you know you had them all out?" She said she asked for the next one, and, finally, nothing came out of the child's mouth.

"Are all of you out of there?" The boy just sat there looking at her, and she asked, "What is your name?" He told her his name. She said, "Are you free of all demons?" He shook his head yes.

"Now, we need to get you baptized in the Holy Ghost. Your house is clean, but those demons will come back with seven times more just like them or worse." She laid hands on him and commanded him to receive the Holy Ghost, and he started speaking in tongues.

I would have loved that. I love to cast out devils. It's fun. When I went back home for a vacation in 1961, my younger sister, Judy, had a demon. She didn't like me because she thought I was too big and bossy, and she didn't want to do what I said when Mama left me in charge.

One day, she came into the living room with a twelve-inch butcher knife and vicious eyes. I looked at her and said, "Demon, you come out in Jesus' Name!" She shot back against the edge of the door and slid down.

This hairy little thing about two feet tall came out of her. I said, "Out, in Jesus' Name!" It went through the screen. It didn't tear the screen, but I could see the screen bulge as it passed through it. So I know demons are real.

If you knew what they looked like, you would be shocked that you were fighting with these things. It'd really be a laughing matter. Now, there are high, more powerful demons, but even a kid who is saved has power over them.

This next miracle of Sister Laura's might seem less important, but not if you were the woman with the problem. There was a woman at Azusa who had a rather unique issue—she burped a lot. She was too embarrassed to go to one of the men, so she found Sister Laura. The woman said she tried to take medicine for it but nothing worked.

"How long have you been burping?" Laura asked.

"For about fifteen years." She said she was at a family reunion and ate a kind of soup. Then she started burping. About every five or six minutes, she burped.

"Oh, well this is an easy one, I think."

Sister Laura laid hands on the woman under her neck, then on her stomach, and prayed for her. "Come back tomorrow and tell me if you've stopped burping."

The woman came back about an hour later and said, "I haven't burped." She came back the next night and told Sister Laura, "I haven't burped. It feels so good!"

Not long into our talk, I would ask the same question of Sister Laura that I asked of every saint: "What was the greatest miracle or healing you personally were a part of?" Sister Laura would tell me about one of the most exciting miracles she participated in—and one of the most exciting miracles ever at Azusa.

Here's the story: A woman came into the meeting holding a staff. She could hardly breathe and looked like a skeleton. She only lived about two miles from Azusa and had started walking to Azusa about three in the afternoon but didn't reach the warehouse until six in the evening. She literally took one baby step at a time, placing the staff in front of her, then scooting her feet up to it and repeating the slow, tedious process until she reached the revival meeting.

She reminded me of the woman in the Bible who knew that if she just touched the hem of the garment of Jesus, she would be healed. That evening at Azusa, this woman was determined to get healed. She came in and looked around as if she were studying the room. At some point, her eyes met Laura's, and she said, "That's the woman I want to pray for me," pointing to Sister Laura.

Sister Laura walked over to her and said, "Mother, what can I do for you?" The next words the lady spoke were almost haunting. "I won't live through the night if God doesn't heal me; I'll die. Doctors say my lungs are ate up with cancer, and I can hardly breathe. I've been losing weight for about a year."

This dear, feeble, elderly woman weighed about sixty-five pounds, standing at about 5'6" tall. She was nothing but bones. Sister Laura laid hands on her and prayed for her.

Immediately, she was able to breathe normally. In the next three hours, she gained a remarkable forty pounds while at the meeting, yet she ate nothing and only breathed in the Shekinah Glory. She said, "My lungs are not hurting; I can breathe like when I was young!"

Yes, there was a great celebration that evening. Sister Laura was a shouter. Her glory bun shook loose and hairpins flew everywhere as she celebrated with this dear saint.

If this were the end of the story, it would be memorable to say the least. However, it is not. Soon after her visit to the warehouse, this lady visited her doctor by the name of Thomas Wyatt. When she entered his office, he asked her to fill out the forms for first-time patients—he did not recognize her. When she told him who she was, he could not believe she was the same person.

After running some tests and checking her out, he told her that her insides were just like new—lungs and all. In amazement, he told her, "There is no way you could have gained that much weight back since the last time I saw you. It is impossible!"

She boldly replied, "I know I couldn't, but God could."

Dr. Wyatt exclaimed, "You're going down to that warehouse, aren't you?"

After attending the revival with her, in a few months he was no longer practicing traditional medicine! Dr. Wyatt founded "Wings of Healing" where he experienced miracles galore. He told the saints at Azusa that the woman cured of cancer and lung failure should have died six months earlier. Truly, her faith not only made her whole but also sustained her on her determined journey to find God and His miraculous power waiting for her at Azusa.

This story gets even better. In 2007, after my first book was published, I received a phone call one day. A woman on the other end said, "Brother Tommy?"

I said, "Yes, this is Brother Tommy."

She said, "The story of the woman with the staff—that was my grandmother."

Now, this woman herself was in her upper eighties, and she was crying. "We used to sit around the table, and grandma would tell us her story of going to Azusa Street with that staff."

"Really?" I was amazed.

She said, "Yes. Some people are trying to say that Dr. Wyatt wasn't really there at Azusa. People are trying to discredit the story."

She said, "Don't let them kid you, Tommy. Don't believe them." Through tears, she continued, "My married name is Wyatt. I married Thomas Wyatt's grandson. Thomas Wyatt *was* my grandmother's doctor."

How do you like that? The granddaughter of the lady with the staff married the doctor's grandson! Still emotional, this woman said, "I just wanted you to know that was my grandmother." Then she hung up. I wanted to talk with her more, but my old phone didn't capture her number, and she was gone. What an ending to that story.

Sister Lucille and Sister Laura, both very wealthy, found something at Azusa that money couldn't buy. They found a common bond forged by heaven in that warehouse. That bonded friendship was still strong and unbreakable sixty years later.

7

GO INTO ALL THE WORLD

Say Hello to Brother Fox

❧

AZUSA AGE: 18

Azusa was a divine training grounds, a heavenly boot camp, of "Your kingdom come. Your will be done" led by God Himself (Matt. 6:10 NKJV). The world came to Azusa seeking healing and returned to their native lands renewed, inspired, transformed and ready to be used of God.

God used this great outpouring not only to meet immediate needs but also to prepare people to serve the needs of His children throughout the world. He brought young people there to train them for the mission field both at home and across the globe. Young and old alike discovered the boundless power of God and how to be used of Him to perform the works of His will.

One such youth was Brother Fox. When he was in his late teenage years, he went to Azusa in preparation to go to the mission field, in particular to India, and labor for God. By the time he arrived at Azusa, Ralph Riggs was about fourteen and C.W. Ward was around sixteen. Brother Fox experienced and participated in the miracles and healings at the warehouse for about eighteen months. By the time he reached his twentieth birthday, he was using what he had learned at Azusa to bring the mighty life-changing power of God to India.

When I met Brother Fox in 1963, he had just retired and settled at Pisgah, renewing his special friendships with many Azusa saints. He was in his early seventies, stood around 5'9" tall, and weighed about 150 pounds. He kept his shiny silver hair kind of long and combed straight back. His hair was so shiny that when he got around a light, it would glow.

I had the privilege of riding with him on a trolley from time to time when he would go and witness to those riding the cable cars. In between his witnessing, I would listen to his stories about India as we traveled. But when it came to stories about Azusa, I went to his apartment, settled at his feet with my cookies and milk and listened intently.

He shared with me that he was awestruck by the movement of God and how the manifestation of God's power varied according to the degree of the manifestation of the Shekinah Glory—the thicker the cloud, the greater the miracles. He was also in awe of Brother Seymour, a very deep man of God.

Fox was present at some of God's most creative miracles through Seymour. Brother Fox heard from God that he himself would have miracles like Seymour's, but in a foreign country—a word that proved itself over and over again as Brother Fox labored in India. Fox took the anointing with him when he left Azusa, but he could not take with him the Shekinah Glory. He explained to me that as far as he could tell, the Shekinah Glory was unique to the Azusa Street Revival.

While at Azusa, Brother Fox went around being used by God to heal everybody he could. He had a special love for the deaf and the mute. He would pray for them and whisper in each ear, "You deaf spirit, you come out in the Name of Jesus." He said he could hear a little pop and "whishing" sound as the ear would be healed. He would then go to the next person and do the same.

If someone couldn't talk, he laid hands on his or her neck. He said, "I'm not one of those who would stick my hand down their mouths—they might get excited and bite a finger off." He told me that he prayed in the Name of Jesus and sometimes they would start talking. Most of the time, though, they would have to learn how to talk but would start making audible sounds.

Brother Fox remembered a man with his neck blackened by a cancer that had eaten up his throat, leaving him unable to talk. Fox prayed for him, laying hands on the lump that protruded from his neck. Looking down at the blackened area after the prayer, Brother Fox said, "I don't see anything happening; something is wrong here." He asked the man, "Are you believing?"

The man nodded his head.

"Let's do it again." With those words, Brother Fox prayed again. This time when he took his hands away, the blackness and lump were gone. He commanded the man, "Talk!"

The man blurted out, "I can't!"

Fox said, "Say that again."

The man realized that a miracle had taken place, and he could talk. The cancer was gone, and his throat was restored. Immediately the man started rejoicing and shouting. Brother Fox just stood there, being the reserved gentleman that he was, in awe of the miracle, with a wide smile on his face.

God was preparing Brother Fox for great and mighty works in India. One lesson he was taught by the Spirit was that you didn't have to heal people one at a time. He recalled when a sign language teacher brought his class of totally deaf people to the meeting.

"If you want to teach them to sign, why did you bring them here? You're going to be out of a job because these people are going to be healed tonight." Brother Fox took the teacher by surprise.

The teacher, obviously unconcerned about job security, responded with apparent disbelief, "You're talking like they are all going to be able to hear."

"They are! They all are going to be healed!" Brother Fox spoke, emboldened by God's Spirit.

This was a group of around thirty-five deaf people. Without wavering, Brother Fox gestured and told them all to join hands and form a circle. He looked at the teacher standing nearby, and told the teacher, "Evidently you don't have much faith, so stand off to the side."

"Now, I'm going to lay hands on this man and start with him." Immediately, Fox realized that they couldn't understand a word he was saying, and the teacher was laughing at him because he too understood that they couldn't hear him. Without hesitation, Brother Fox simply whispered in the first man's ear and told the spirit to come out. The miracle was immediate.

As soon as the once-deaf man could hear, he got excited. When the others saw his excitement and that he could hear, they started getting healed one by one like a line of dominoes—in just a few minutes all of them were healed and the teacher was jobless.

Fox had only touched the first man in the circle. From that point on, God took over and allowed His power to flow through the connected hands touching each and every one gathered in the circle.

I sat and listened to Brother Fox tell his stories both about Azusa and India and the mighty miracles God used him to perform. I couldn't help but remember the words recorded in John 14:12. Jesus told His disciples, "He who believes in Me, the works that I do he will do also; and greater works than these he will do..." (NKJV).

Brother Fox trained at Azusa in Kingdom work and brought the Spirit of God to India. There the blind found sight, the lame could walk, the sick became healthy and miraculous healings were commonplace. The only thing he lacked was the Shekinah Glory.

8

BLINDED BY THE LIGHT

Say Hello to Brother Brown

AZUSA AGE: 16

"Forget the past and look forward to what is ahead." In Philippians 3:13, Paul talked about not looking back at the past. Could you imagine how debilitating it would have been to Paul to look back at who he was or what he had done? Looking back, whether on things bad or good, can cripple the present and disable the future.

Dear Brother Brown was a good example of this. I met Bill Brown in 1960. He had arrived and retired at Pisgah just about six months before my arrival. When I met him, he stood several inches over six feet, had a medium build and weighed around 200 pounds.

He lived in the dormitory with me and constantly wanted to talk about Azusa. In fact, that is all he wanted to talk about. From time to time we would go down to the dining hall together, and he would be in "heaven" as he got a chance to re-live his days at Azusa.

At Azusa, Brother Brown loved ministering to those who were blind. He shared with me that while there, he participated in the healing of more than fifty blind people, and each and every time the healing was instantaneous.

I asked Brother Brown if any particular healing stood out in his mind, and he shared the story of a woman whose eyes were totally dark, almost black, with no white showing anywhere. The whites of her eyes had never developed; she had been blind from birth. The reason this miracle stood out in his memory is that when she opened her eyes after he prayed for her and she realized she could see, the lady let out a loud, bloodcurdling scream that caused him to jump back in momentary fear. Brother Brown said he was just about ready to start shouting himself, but her scream was so sudden and unexpected it caught him by surprise. After the shock wore off, they both began to rejoice.

All of his miracles were not with the blind. He participated in miracles for the crippled, deformed and those confined to wheelchairs due to illness or physical disabilities. He recalled one time going up to a man who was lying on a cot. Brother Brown asked him, "Do you want to be healed? Do you want to take up your cot and carry it home?"

The man looked up and smiled. "Yes." His response was simple, but clear. Brother Bill prayed for him, and immediately he got up, folded his cot, then walked away from it and paraded around worshipping God.

Before the man left the meeting, he went back to where he had been confined to the cot, picked it up and carried it away while rejoicing that he had been healed.

While Sister Carney and Brothers Ward, Riggs and Anderson were running around seeking out people to minister to, Brother Brown was more subdued. Being more of a loner, he wandered around looking mostly for blind people to whom he could minister.

After the departure of the Shekinah Glory, for the next several years, Brother Brown would return to the Azusa Street warehouse where Seymour still preached. He didn't go there with anticipation of seeing God move miraculously. Rather, he returned moping around, mourning what had been. He would sit in the service and weep for the loss of yesterday.

When I met him decades later, he told me that he had spent a lifetime remembering Azusa, but never moving on. He would wistfully tell me that he should have been preaching the Gospel, or that he should have been a missionary like Brother Fox or Brother Lake. At least two great denominations, The Assemblies of God and The Church of God in Christ, were born out of Azusa by leaders such as Ralph Riggs, C.W. Ward and Charles Harrison Mason.

Regretfully, he told me, he had missed God's purpose or will for his life. For over fifty years he lived in the past, sitting around daydreaming about the yesteryears of Azusa. Wasted years!

Now retired with his productive years behind him, he settled among the saints of Azusa where he could share his stories with those who would understand and re-live with him the Azusa legacy. But when old Brother Brown wasn't sharing his past, I would sometimes see him sitting around Pisgah, tears coming down his face as he cried over the loss of the Shekinah Glory.

"It's coming back, Bill," I'd say to him. "Remember the hundred-year prophecy?"

He'd nod and say, "Yes, but I won't be here. In forty or fifty years, I won't be here."

Often I would leave my meeting with Brother Brown feeling bittersweet. I shared his joy of all that Azusa was, but I felt helpless when faced with the lingering melancholy of this dear brother. How could one who had been used of God to heal so many who were blind, been so blind himself?

9

GOD OF THE LITTLE THINGS

Say Hello to Brother Cantrell

Azusa Age: 21

Brother Cantrell was the one who always messed up my hairdo when he prayed for me. But every time he prayed, I was healed. Brother Cantrell was of moderate height, standing 5'9", so he had to reach up a bit to get to the top of my 6'2" head.

I vividly recall that he wore a hat all the time except when he was in church. Even though he was single, he baked fresh cookies and always had cold milk waiting for me for our long talks. Once a month I would go to his apartment, which was diagonal from Pisgah. When he told me his stories, I sat at Brother Cantrell's feet on a throw rug, and he sat in an upholstered chair.

Even when he told his stories, he never showed much emotion. He was pleasant, nice and friendly, but not big on emotions.

When our meetings first started, I asked him if he personally had had any great miracles. He replied, "Anyone who attended Azusa very long had great miracles—especially if a person attended at least once a week—you had miracles!"

"In fact," Brother Cantrell said, "God taught me a valuable lesson at Azusa. There was a man there who started quacking like a duck after receiving the Baptism of the Holy Spirit. I thought that the man was making a mockery of the Baptism, and I got upset with him. I thought, 'This is not a language.'"

"Many years later in the 1930s, I saw a documentary about a tribe in a place called Quackland. Their language was just like that of a duck. I realized that I was upset with this poor man and all he did was speak in the language of Quackland. I have learned since never to question the acts of God, no matter how unique the act is."

Unique is definitely the word for the next miracle I remember Brother Cantrell telling me. There was a man who came to Brother Cantrell who had been hiccupping for twenty-three years. Twenty-three years!

"I don't know why. All of a sudden, I started hiccupping," the man said. About every minute this poor guy would hiccup, and he'd keep on talking and hiccupping. He wanted to become a country western singer when the hiccupping started. He couldn't pursue his dream.

Brother Cantrell said, "Boy, I'd hate that. That's terrible."

So he put his hands on this man's back and on his chest and prayed for him. The man came back later and said, "How long have I been here?"

Brother Cantrell said, "I don't know—at least a couple of hours."

He said, "I haven't hiccupped. I haven't hiccupped for two hours!" He was completely delivered of such a seemingly little thing, the hiccups. But just imagine hiccupping every minute for all those years. Not such a little thing after all.

I asked Brother Cantrell to tell me about his most interesting miracle. He sat almost emotionless and told the story of the man who was what Cantrell called "tongue-tied." The man was in his late twenties, and instead of talking, he just mumbled. Brother Cantrell couldn't understand a word he said and finally told the man, "Let's stop talking and get you healed so I can understand you."

The man nodded his head and Brother Cantrell laid hands on him and told him to stick his tongue out. The man gestured that he couldn't, so Brother Cantrell reached down in the man's mouth and touched his tongue.

In an authoritative voice, he commanded, "In the Name of Jesus, tongue, I command you to be free." And miraculously he was able to stick his tongue out. Brother Cantrell looked at the man's tongue, now loosed, and asked the man, "Can you talk now?"

The man said, "I don't know." Then he realized that he was talking in a normal voice and got all excited. He ran shouting, "Glory, hallelujah!" He could speak perfectly. He didn't have to learn how to talk; he just needed his tongue loosed.

Brother Cantrell was personally involved in one or two miracles a week, but he observed thousands of miracles performed over the years. He was just about twenty-one years old himself but told me that he loved to watch teenagers like Riggs, Ward, Anderson, and Carney. They would be running around having an exciting time, smiles on their faces, and praying for people as God supernaturally worked miracles through them.

This man of God continued to be a vessel of God's love throughout his life. He preached for decades with the Foursquare Church and worked with Aimee Semple McPherson. I never saw him frown or laugh, but a smile graced his face at all times.

10

GOOD AND FAITHFUL SERVANT

Say Hello to Sister Goldie

AZUSA AGE: 18

Sister Goldie is special to me. She was the one who bee-lined it for me that day on Venice Beach. She was the one God used to lead me to Christ as my personal Savior. She was the one who opened up the world of Azusa Street to me when she brought me to live with the saints at Pisgah. I must have been special to her as well because she introduced me to people as her son. I'd just smile at them. Truth is, she was like a mother to me and spoiled me. She bought my first Bible for me with my name on it. She even bought my first dress coat and dress shoes.

Sister Goldie lived at Venice Beach but came to Pisgah once a month. She always arrived early so she could tell me her stories. Faithful to the tradition that was common among the saints, she brought her homemade chocolate chip cookies and cold milk that she had purchased from Dick's Market after she got off the bus. With cookies and cold milk in hand, she would walk down to Pisgah.

We would meet in the back of the dining hall where there were couches and chairs. At first it was just the two of us, but after a few months she began to draw an audience of young people and adults who just wanted to hear her stories about the mighty works of God. She needed very little coaxing. One of the main reasons she came to Pisgah each month was to tell her stories, and she loved the opportunity to re-live those moments she spent serving God at Azusa.

In 1908 when she was about eighteen years old, she started attending the Azusa Revival, and attended for about two years. She was already a Christian and didn't need healing, but she wanted to be a part of what was happening. Sister Goldie observed Sister Carney for a few days—what she did and how she did it—then looked for people to bless on her own.

Sister Goldie was drawn to people with obvious disfigurements. One such young man had a bow in his arm. He had broken his arm in a ballgame at school several years prior. For some reason he never saw a doctor, and the bones had never been reset. She looked at the man and said, "This is going to be fun."

The young man looked at her and said, "It's going to be what?"

"It's going to be fun," she repeated.

She took his deformed arm in one hand and touched the bowed bones with her other hand. She looked straight at the arm and said, "I take all authority over you, and I command you in the Name of Jesus, straighten out!" Immediately and miraculously, the arm straightened and healed—no noise, no popping—and quietly became normal.

Now, one day in late 1907, a woman in her mid-forties came in the church and waddled up to Sister Goldie. That's right, waddled. Like a penguin. "How long have you been like this?" Goldie asked.

"It started in my teens, but not badly. Now look at me. It's like my feet won't quit turning." They were so turned out they were almost facing the other direction. She could hardly walk even with the help of a crude walker. They didn't have many at the time.

"Oh, my. We've got to stop this right now. Let's get into prayer." Sister Goldie prayed, "God, I don't want this to be a slow one. I want this woman to be healed." Everyone nearby yelled, "In Jesus' Name!"

They watched and waited. Nothing. The woman started to talk, but Goldie hushed her. "Be quiet. Watch, watch!" Then, all of a sudden, they heard little pops. Her feet slowly untwisted. When they were straight, the woman said, "That's enough! That's enough!" She didn't want to become pigeon-toed.

Sister Goldie said, "Sister, can you walk now?"

"No," she said.

"Well, leave that little walker here with me." The woman started walking, and she walked a few feet and came back. Goldie encouraged her. "Now, try to walk a little faster."

Pretty soon, Goldie and that woman were running a race around Azusa Street. Running! The woman kept coming back to the church, perfectly whole.

Of course, her hubby soon came back with her. He wanted to see what was going on because he had a liver disease called cirrhosis, which causes the liver not to work properly. Naturally, they wanted to see Sister Goldie.

Sister Goldie warned him before she prayed for him. "Now, if I do anything odd, just leave it alone. Do you want to be healed?"

"Yes," he said.

She laid her hands over his liver area.

Just before she called upon Jesus, she drew her right fist back and then commanded, "Be healed, in Jesus' Name!" Thwack! She punched him squarely in the chest. He told her it hurt, but he seemed to have no problems from then on.

He went to his doctor for a confirmation. "We don't understand this," the doctor said. "It's like you have the liver of an eighteen-year-old." God had given him a new liver! The doctor said, "Now, stop your smoking and drinking." Of course, he did.

They both became workers in churches. I thought that sock-it-to-'em approach sounded more like Allan or Cole or Jaggers. I asked, "Why did you hit him in the chest?"

"God said, 'Hit him in the chest.' He didn't say swat him. He said hit him." Sister Goldie was matter-of-fact. "So I doubled up my fist, and I hit him."

As I mentioned, Sister Goldie was drawn to people who had disfigurements or ugly growths on their faces and would pray for them. Most people just tolerated small growths on their faces and didn't seek healing. But Sister Goldie had other thoughts. She'd tell them, "God can clean this up. That's a mess. That's ugly, and God doesn't want you being a mess or ugly."

After the first couple of healings where the growths or tumors just fell off in her hand, she began to carry towels and a dustpan with her. Sometimes she had to bandage the area where the growth had been because the tumors or growths would come off and leave a wound in the flesh. Sometimes the total miracle was not instantaneous. The tumor would come off, but the complete healing would take hours—even overnight.

She remembered examining this large tumor that fell off of this woman after she prayed for her. "You could see little black things in there working."

Sister Goldie believed it was cancer—live, malignant cancer, so powerful that it was splitting and wiggling and moving.

Sister Goldie was instrumental in healing perhaps 3,000 tumors and facial growths during the two years she attended the revival services.

From Azusa to Venice Beach, from 1908 until her death, this dear saint was found faithfully serving God with each and every gift and ability He had entrusted to her. When she went to be with the Lord, I am certain she heard the words from Matthew 25:23: "Well done, my good and faithful servant."

11

A SWEET, SWEET SONG

Say Hello to Brother Jonah

AZUSA AGE: 30s

This story is a bit different from the rest. The man who received the miracle told me his own story. His name was Brother Jonah, and I met him in at Pisgah in 1962.

When I met Brother Jonah, he wasn't really sure of his age because he was illegitimate and had no birth certificate. But he was somewhere in his nineties at Pisgah, which made him in his thirties when he came to Azusa Street in 1909.

God had called Jonah to preach the Gospel. There was only one problem. "God, I can't preach the Bible until I'm able to read the Bible. I can't read or write, and You know it," Jonah complained to God one day. So Brother Jonah came to Azusa, and Brother Seymour laid hands on and prayed for him.

Jonah heard God say to him, "Pick up the Bible, open it and start reading." He picked up the Bible, turned to the first page and, all of a sudden, understood everything he read.

He went through the Bible in about a week. After that, he couldn't read anymore.

I could ask him any question concerning the Bible, and he'd quote me the verse. I could say, "What about in the Book of Habakkuk?" He'd quote it to me word for word and never missed anything.

When Jonah preached, he did not talk. He sang. The first time I heard him, he said, "I am going to be preaching today on adultery, and there are several men and a couple of women in here who need to come to the altar." He turned to his daughter who worked with him and said, "Now, baby, you start playing this."

She started playing a certain tune on the piano, and he sang to it. He started in Genesis, singing, and he sang every scripture on adultery from Genesis to Revelation. Then he looked around and said, "Now, you who are in the sin of adultery, if you don't repent, you're gonna go to hell. Some of you will die soon if you don't come up here."

I watched about twelve men and four women come to the altar. A few of them shocked me. What really amazed me, though, was how Brother Jonah remembered the entire Bible...and only after reading it once! His musical approach to preaching was also pretty unique.

12

COLOR BLIND

Say Hello to Brother Garcia

 ❦

Azusa Age: 18

Openness of worship and acceptance of every person regardless of race was one of the critical factors that led David Garcia, a young Mexican-American, to attend services at Azusa every evening after work, as well as Saturdays and Sundays. He liked ministering to the Hispanics who would come to the services. If he saw no one tending to them, he'd go over and start praying for them.

I met Brother David at Pisgah where he had lived since about 1955. He stood 5'7" tall and weighed about 200 pounds. Brother Smith told me, "About once a month, David will do a dance that's supernatural."

I asked, "Oh, what's supernatural about it?"

Smith said, "He will dance all around this church, and his eyes will be tightly shut."

I said, "I've got to see that."

Brother David sat in the middle of the church, in the middle of the row of seats. One night during worship, he suddenly started bouncing.

As if on cue, everybody left the aisle he was in and stood back to see which way he'd go.

After bouncing, he broke into this wild run, legs moving crazily. I thought of Crazylegs Hirsch. His arms were flinging every which way. His eyes were tightly shut. Everybody made a clear path for him.

He made about three laps around the church and down the aisles, and then he stopped exactly where he started. He looked around, went back to his seat and sat down.

Afterwards I asked him, "Brother David, do you know what's happening when you're dancing?"

"Yeah, I'm having a great time."

I asked, "But do you know what you're doing?"

He said, "No. My eyes are closed. I just feel myself moving." He just enjoyed the pleasantness of it.

At the time of Azusa, David was around eighteen years old and lived just about a mile from the warehouse. He started attending the revival shortly after the meetings began in 1906.

When we got together to talk about Azusa, Brother Garcia broke tradition and served strong coffee rather than cold milk and cookies. That was basically the only difference as I sat at his feet in respect and listened to him re-live his memories of God's mighty works.

Brother David began with the story of the Grand Central Station experience. David lived about a half mile on the other side of Grand Central Station and walked right by it coming to the Azusa Street warehouse. One evening he ran to the meeting to find Frank Bartleman and told him that he needed to come to Grand Central Station.

"Why? What's going on there?" Bartleman asked out of curiosity.

Brother Garcia, while trying to catch his breath, exclaimed, "You've got to come and see this! The anointing is far beyond where it has been in the past. You have to come on down and see!"

Together, Bartleman and Garcia ran down to the station that was a half mile away from the warehouse. There they witnessed people come in from all over the world, get off the train, walk across the platform and fall out in the Spirit, often speaking in tongues. Someone had commented that the phenomenon had been happening all day long.

When Garcia first saw the people lying all over the platform area, he thought it was a disaster until he realized what was going on and ran to find Bartleman. Frank had talked about a line or circle of blood—several blocks around the Azusa warehouse—where the power of God extended outward.

Several blocks before reaching the warehouse, people were being healed, falling out in the Spirit and speaking in tongues for the first time. This was the first time God's power had reached all the way to Grand Central Station. Although no miracles were taking place, the Presence and power of God, without question, had now moved out a half mile from the actual warehouse!

Brother Garcia was also awestruck by the Shekinah Glory that lingered for over three years in and around the warehouse. During the day, he could sometimes see a glowy steam coming from the building. He would tell me, "We have got to get the Shekinah back if we want to see a worldwide revival!"

I asked Brother David, "Did you ever see the flames?"

He told me how he'd get off work during the wintertime, and it would be dark. He'd take the bus home, shower, and come out on his porch, looking across the Arroyo Seco River. Some nights he could see the flames shooting up fifty feet into the sky and coming down out of the sky. He said, "Brother Tommy, I'd run the whole way. I didn't walk. I ran, shouting, 'Glory hallelujah,' because big things were happening at Azusa when those flames were there."

He wanted to be a part of it all.

He explained that the experience of the Shekinah Glory was greater than breathing pure oxygen. It was heaven's breath. There were times the mist was only a foot high, and he would lie down in it to breathe in God's Glory.

Brother Garcia often stressed that the greater the Shekinah Glory, the greater the power. He would note that the flames were there when

God, through Seymour, performed the mightiest of miracles, where a leg grew out and another where an arm grew out where there was none before.

Garcia was there when the arm grew out. He said, "Brother Tommy, this man didn't have a ball joint in his shoulder; it had been ripped out. I was close enough to be looking right at the shoulder.

"All of a sudden, I saw the bones start to come out, and then flesh started coming around them. This man's arm just shot out in what seemed mere seconds as I watched." For Garcia, it seemed like he was watching this miracle in slow motion as he was awed at what God was doing.

Brother Garcia was the first to tell me of Seymour's prophecy that in about one hundred years there would be a return of the Shekinah Glory and a revival that would surpass the works of God at Azusa. When we talked in the 1960s, Garcia realized that the prophecy was still forty years away from being fulfilled, but still longed for God to accelerate His plans and allow the Shekinah Glory to fall again in his lifetime.

I loved to hear about the cloud or mist that filled Azusa, signifying the Presence of God. I also loved to hear about the great miracles that happened in that mist. I would ask Brother David to describe the greatest miracle he had ever participated in.

Without hesitation, he would tell of the multiple healings that took place all within a few minutes. There were two women and a man all with crippling arthritis who couldn't walk. They were in wheelchairs and had come from a nearby nursing home. One of the women couldn't even feed herself. Brother Garcia asked, "Did you come to get healed?" All three said yes or nodded their heads. Sister Carney lifted up the footrests on all the wheelchairs in preparation for what was about to happen.

First Garcia laid hands on the head of the lady who couldn't feed herself and couldn't even talk, and prayed for her. Immediately her head quit shaking. She looked up at Brother David and said, "Are you Jesus?"

Brother Garcia laughed and said, "No, Jesus is in me, and I prayed for you in the Name of Jesus, but I'm not Jesus. But Jesus just healed you!"

She looked at him for a long time and finally said, "Can I get up?"

Garcia smiled and said, "Yes, I told you in the Name of Jesus, get up and walk!"

The once-crippled lady got up and started walking and then started doing a waltz-type dance—a beautiful dance as if she were a young woman. She danced for at least an hour.

Brother Garcia smiled and watched her dance in delight. Then he looked around at the other woman. With a knowing smile on her face, she simply said, "I'm ready."

He came over and prayed for her, and in a minute she was up. She kind of stood there shaking, as if she were afraid. Brother David reached out to steady her, but she said, "No, leave me alone; pray for him."

Brother Garcia turned to the man and prayed for him. The crippled man asked, "What is this? It's like electricity."

Garcia simply replied, "It's the power of God. You're healed in the Name of Jesus, and you can get up and walk or run or dance or whatever you want to do."

I asked, "Well, what did he do?"

Garcia replied, "He took off in a streak, running, as I just stood there marveling at all three of them celebrating their healings."

Brother David then would tell me his most endearing miracle. A little Hispanic girl, about the age of six, was blind. Her eyes were gray—a scary-looking gray. Her parents told him that she started going blind at about the age of two and was completely blind by the time she was four.

He prayed for the child, and when she opened her eyes, the gray was gone, replaced with beautiful black eyes. She had been instantly healed. The child started dancing and celebrating, screaming the Name of Jesus while her parents tried to keep up with her.

Brother Garcia also recalled a man in his mid-thirties who had a gum disease. His face was almost a dark red due to the poison in his gums, which were a blackish color because of his teeth rotting. He laid hands on the man and prayed, and then told him to open his mouth. He asked the man if he felt anything and the man replied, "Yeah. I feel something."

Brother Garcia said, "I don't think so. You didn't feel anything because nothing happened here. Close your mouth again." Garcia prayed a second time and asked, "Feeling anything?"

"A little."

Garcia replied, "We're not getting it done." Before he prayed a third time, he asked, "Do you believe God is going to give you new gums and new teeth, and He's going to clear up this infection in your face? Do you understand that is what we're praying for? You're going to get healed."

In obedience, the man said, "Okay."

Garcia prayed and this time the redness disappeared from the man's face. When the man opened his mouth, his gums were turning pink, and to Garcia's astonishment, he saw rotten teeth heal. By the time the man left the meeting that evening, he was completely healed!

I had the privilege of meeting the man's son, Bill, at Pisgah when Brother Smith introduced him to me. I had several conversations with Bill and finally asked the question I was dying to ask. "Bill," I said, "did your dad have bad teeth when he died?" Bill just grinned at the question and told me that in fact, at the time of his death, his dad had a full set of perfect teeth in his head.

The most astonishing miracle Brother David described to me was of the man whose stomach had split open and his entrails dangled out of a hole. The man had a cloth covering it. David picked up the cloth and looked at eighteen to twenty inches of the man's insides on the outside of his body. "Dear God, this stinks!" he said.

The man said, "It's been this way for about a year." David said he thought to himself, "Dear God, how is he still alive?"

He put the cloth back down and laid his hands on the grotesque wound. As he prayed, he watched his hand "travel back" to the man's stomach. Brother David said, "I didn't know what to do. I just stood with my hand on his stomach. Finally I stopped and picked up that rag. There was no hole. It was just like it had never been there."

Brother Garcia summed up his experience with God at Azusa with these words: "When you came into Azusa, you got healed. The more you attended, the more faith you had, and the more things would happen. Because your faith was building up as you saw other people believing, you soon had no doubt when you walked up to someone that he or she was going to get healed. After a while, it was easy to have the boldness to walk up to anyone and proclaim, 'God is going to heal you tonight!'" There was no room for any seed of doubt in this fertile soil of faith.

13

LEGS TO STAND ON

Say Hello to Sister Mangrum

ᑍᕔ

Azusa Age: 22

Sister Mangrum enjoyed a special privilege. She not only possessed blessed memories from Azusa Street, but she also looked at and lived with one of her miracles every day. God healed many people through Sister Mangrum's ministry at Azusa. Her most special miracle story involved the healing of a lady who was in her mid-forties during the revival. I considered it an honor that I got to meet this woman as she neared her hundredth birthday.

"Mother" Mangrum, as she was later called, was in her early twenties at Azusa but in her mid-seventies when I met her at Pisgah. She stood around 5'2" and weighed about 110 pounds. She was always very well dressed, very prim and proper, well-spoken, as well as kind and courteous.

Mother Mangrum often called me her "little" boy, and I had the honor of going once a month to her home, which was one of the larger apartments on the grounds. As tradition would dictate, she would bake chocolate chip cookies and serve cold milk during our time together. I sat on a huge throw rug that almost covered the entire floor. She sat on a good-sized, antique, wooden rocking chair that had belonged to her great-grandmother. Mother Mangrum was part of the "Carney" crowd and, like Sister Carney, was married at the time of Azusa and attended the revival services with her husband.

One of Mother Mangrum's favorite stories was about the pigeon-toed woman. She was in her mid-forties and couldn't walk very well as her knees bowed inward and had been that way since her teenage years. Mother Mangrum immediately noticed her as she came scooting and wobbling in, walking kind of funny. Mother Mangrum went over to her and asked, "Have you come to be healed?"

The lady responded, "I came to see what was going on. You say I can be healed? Of what?"

Mother Mangrum pointed to her legs and said, "Of your legs." She sat down with the woman and tried to convince her that God would straighten up her legs.

The woman responded in a slight stutter, "Well, ah, ah, it's worth a try." She told Mother Mangrum that people had made fun of her since she was young.

Mother Mangrum eagerly responded, "What have you got to lose?" She prayed for her, keeping her hands on the woman's head. She described a heat coming out of her hands onto the woman.

Finally the woman started shaking and said, "Something's happening; something's happening!"

Mother Mangrum looked down at the woman's legs and excitedly told the woman to look. Her feet and legs were straightening out, and in about two minutes she was completely restored. Knees, twisted legs and pigeon-toed feet were totally straightened and healed.

She asked the woman, "Would you like to walk normal now? We could do a dance all over this place."

The woman admitted, "I have never danced in my whole life."

Mother Mangrum smiled and said, "Well, let's learn now," and they began to dance.

Soon the woman realized that a miracle had really happened to her and went "wild" dancing before God. Before Mother Mangrum knew it, the lady had run out of the building and several minutes later came running back in screaming and hollering—she wanted to get back into the building, afraid she might lose her healing if she wasn't inside. After she settled down, she looked around and asked, "What is this stuff?"

"We call it the Shekinah Glory."

While at Pisgah, I got to meet this lady, who by then was nearing a hundred years old.

After the miracle, she gave the rest of her life to ministering to homeless women. For years she operated a rescue mission down on skid row for women on the streets. When I would go to see her, she was all but on her deathbed. Her one question to me and all the saints was, "I just want to know what happened to that Shekinah Glory."

Of course, my curiosity got the best of me, and I asked to see this elderly woman's legs that had been healed. At first she was reluctant, but then with some encouragement from Mother Mangrum, she showed me her legs—still completely healed after all those years. In fact, I felt that Betty Grable's "million dollar legs" had nothing on the legs of this woman whom God had touched. She was living proof right before my eyes that God had visited Azusa in an unprecedented way.

Mother Mangrum always loved to recount the story of the woman with the hooked nose. When she first noticed the lady, Mother Mangrum told me she thought that maybe a doctor could help fix her ugly nose, but God had other ideas. She heard a small voice within her say, "I am a better doctor than any doctor here on earth." With that message from God, she looked at the lady again and felt that she needed to pray for her.

She went to the woman and prayed, but the results were not immediate. Later on in the service, Mother Mangrum noticed that the "hook" was gone and went up to her and commented about the healing.

The woman was somewhat happy but told Mother Mangrum, "I know the hook is gone, but I don't like the little point at the end of my nose." Mother Mangrum understood her concern and prayed for her again, and before the lady left the meeting a few hours later, she had a perfect nose. Looking at God's miracle, Mother Mangrum silently rejoiced as she thought how wonderful it was that God cared enough about a person's feelings to straighten out this lady's ugly nose.

Mother Mangrum was somewhat theatrical when she told her stories and made the stories come alive with her many gestures. One of the most astonishing stories she told me is this next one.

Think of the movies *The Elephant Man* or *The Mask*, and you can picture the total disfigurement of this twenty-five to thirty-year-old man who came to Azusa Street. He came there on his own, pathetically dragging his feet, sickening-looking with one eye shooting up and the other looking down. His mind was perfectly fine, but he had been born deformed, and the condition grew worse and worse. His mouth and jaw hung below his left breast. How he ate, I don't know.

Mother Mangrum made her way over to him, and he looked at her with his twisted eyes and uttered something. "What did you say?" asked Mother Mangrum.

He mumbled, "I came here to get healed."

She said, "Oh, praise God! You're gonna be a great testimony!"

He said, "Okay, I'm ready." I love the fact that he came to Azusa ready.

She slapped hands on him and held them there as his body "danced" under her touch. His face started contorting and coming back together. His jaw withdrew into place, his eyes rotated in their sockets and his back, legs and hands untwisted.

I asked how long it took. She said a very attractive man stood in front of her in about five minutes. Over two decades of deformity were made perfect in five minutes. I never found out his name. He became a minister after God blessed him with this healing.

I believe this miracle alone could start an awakening.

14

WHAT GOD HAS JOINED TOGETHER

Say Hello to Mr. And Mrs. Lankford

❧

AZUSA AGES: 20 AND 18

While most seventeen-year-old boys chase after girls, Brother Lankford pursued God. His hunger for more of God took him from Highland Park, California, to Topeka, Kansas, in 1903. This was the city in which Dr. Charles Parham had started a Bible school where he taught a new concept—the Baptism of the Holy Spirit accompanied by the gift of tongues. Remember, Dr. Parham was Brother Seymour's pastor in Pasadena, Texas.

Under Parham's witness, Brother Lankford received the Baptism and gift himself. Little did Brother Lankford realize how this gift would be used in the very near future and the years to come.

In 1904, at eighteen, he returned to California and introduced this new teaching to Dr. Yoakum, the founder of Pisgah whom you will read about later. After receiving the Baptism and gift of tongues, Dr. Yoakum taught others at Pisgah about this exciting experience.

Brother Lankford and Dr. Yoakum led Sister Carney to receive the Baptism and gift in 1904, two years prior to Azusa.

I had the privilege of getting to know Brother Lankford and Sister Lankford during my time at Pisgah. He stood a few inches taller than six feet, and she stood about 5'10". Mrs. Lankford was soft-spoken and very sweet. On the other hand, Brother Lankford could be gruff at times.

Unlike my other visits, when I came to their home, I wasn't greeted with cookies and milk. Brother Lankford had discovered my weakness for strawberry ice cream, which was also his favorite. So I sat at their feet and enjoyed this pink delight while listening to their stories.

The Lankfords were all about being used by God to bring about healings and miracles. The entire evening was one story after another about the miraculous works of God at Azusa. I would often begin by asking the Lankfords to tell me their most interesting miracles. Once the question left my lips, Brother Lankford would begin, and Mrs. Lankford would add her memories to those of her husband.

Lankford told me about a man who had gotten two fingers caught in some type of machine. Before he knew it, the machine had ripped off two of his fingers. The man had heard that astonishing miracles happened at the warehouse on Azusa Street, so he came with the expectation of getting healed.

Brother Lankford shocked the man by asking, "Can we see what God will do?"

The man, somewhat puzzled, replied, "What do you mean?"

"Let's ask God to grow them out!" Lankford was very bold and outspoken.

With the man's approval, Lankford grabbed the man's hand and instructed him to put it up in the air. Holding the man's hand up high, and with Sister Lankford holding up his arm, Lankford began to pray. The man's fingers began to grow out!

Sister Lankford passed out from the sight of such a miracle. Lankford started taking the man around shouting that his fingers had just grown out. You could hear Lankford cry out, "These weren't here before. Look, God grew these fingers out!"

The man stood next to Lankford in shock with his mouth open in amazement. Before the miracle was over, even the man's fingernails grew in as the man was made whole.

Mrs. Lankford smiled as her husband told about the greatest miracle he had been a part of, and as soon as he finished, she said, "Let me tell you my most memorable miracle."

Sister Lankford didn't wait for approval but began to tell her story. At the time of this miracle, the Lankfords were engaged, and she said somewhat forcefully, "Honey, come here!" He wasn't used to her talking like that because she was very sweet and very soft-spoken. She said, "Look here at this sister of ours whom God is going to heal."

The lady had a very bad hunchback. Her back didn't just curve over; it was twisted. She was probably around fifty to fifty-five years old. She told Sister Lankford that the problem had started when she was about thirty, and it had just gotten worse and worse. The doctor wanted to put her into a nursing home, and even her husband agreed because she could hardly get around. Well, her husband brought her to Azusa, thinking that maybe God would do something at the revival meeting.

Brother Lankford came over and laid his hands on the hunched back and started praying for her. You could hear the popping of the bones. Within minutes, right before their eyes, she was healed. She broke into dancing and even went up onto the platform dancing and screaming.

Right behind her was Brother Anderson, who had been standing up on a bench witnessing the miracle and hearing the bones cracking. I asked Sister Lankford, "What did you and Brother Lankford do?"

She responded, "Well, we were both running with her."

Now it was Brother Lankford's turn. "Another memorable miracle was the crippled man in a wheelchair who wouldn't let the doctors cut off his legs." Lankford went on to explain that the man had worked as a brakeman for the railroad and had been crippled in an accident when a train pinned his legs down and broke many of his bones. You could tell through his pants that the bones in his legs were kind of knotty, but he was too shy or embarrassed to pull up his pant legs to show his injuries.

Brother Lankford declared, "Well, we can't allow that to happen. It's about time you came here."

The man quietly said, "Yes, I'm here."

Lankford said that he wasn't sure if he had come alone, but he had pushed himself into the service.

When Brother Lankford saw him sitting there, he said it brought him to tears. He said to the man, "It's a miracle they didn't cut your legs off."

The crippled man answered, "I have been paralyzed from the waist down for about two years. They wanted to amputate, but I wouldn't let them."

Brother Lankford started praying for him, and Sister Carney, who was observing, broke in and corrected him. "No, no, no, that's not faith!" She went over to the man and picked up his legs and put the footrests up, so he could get up. She expected him to get up!

After Sister Carney was done, Brother Lankford prayed for the man. You could hear the bones cracking and see the legs just straighten up. The man got out of his wheelchair and went flying! Of course, a bunch of those who surrounded the man went with him.

I thought that was an extreme phenomenon. Lankford said, "Yes, God put the bones back together. You could see when the man came to Azusa that he was pathetic—he couldn't walk, and he couldn't move from the waist down. Then here this man was running around the place shouting and dancing and leaping."

I sat there, thinking, "It is no wonder they had such a revival. No wonder this thing went worldwide. Yes, they received the speaking in tongues and that was great, but many of the miracles that were performed were not done by big preachers. Many of those being used by God were just ordinary teenagers and young people doing extraordinary works through God."

Brother Lankford also was blessed with the great gift of helping people who had cleft palates or lips to receive healing. The majority of them were children. Some of those who came there for healing had never had operations or medical treatment. There would be big gaps in their mouths, and he would pray for them and the gaps would be filled in. Sometimes some of their teeth would be gone and the teeth would be restored.

I said, "Teeth and all?"

Brother Lankford nodded and said, "Teeth and all."

Lankford said that over the three-year period he was there, God used him in healing around a hundred people with cleft palates. Because most of them were just kids, he became known as "papa" to the children he healed. When they'd come back to see him, he was papa.

Now, this is the first time I've dared to tell this next story. It may make a listener or reader blush, but it's fresh in my mind. A couple came in one day, and the wife was very upset, even to the point of divorce. When Brother Lankford asked what was the problem, the wife complained that they couldn't have sex anymore. Her husband was impotent.

This couple was in their seventies, but that was no matter—she wanted intimacy. She didn't want him to stop being a man. She needed a man. Brother Lankford said, "Oh, that can't happen. That's wrong. No. That shouldn't die." See, the Lankfords were older when they told me this story, and they were still very intimate. "That's the devil," he said to the man.

He laid hands on the man and ordered that spirit to leave him and for him to be healed enough to make his wife happy. That was it. A few nights later, the couple came back. She said, "Oh, my, my. He's more frisky than he was when we first got married!"

Brother Lankford said, "It was the devil wanting to break you two up. I just cast it off him."

She said, "My! God works any miracle." These people were married, and God wanted them to stay that way.

Mrs. Lankford wanted to continue with more stories, but Brother Lankford wasn't quite finished. "Two more stories. Let me tell you about the tumor on the spine. Even though the tumor was covered by the man's shirt, you could see the outline of the tumor. It stood out about three inches, and was about a foot long, and four inches wide."

Brother Lankford described the man as middle-aged and, according to the man, the tumor had been there for about three years. The man came in with a bunch of people, and someone let Brother Lankford know about him. The next day he was to have x-rays taken to find out what was wrong. Lankford told how he prayed over the tumor, and it just sank into the man's body. The man was totally healed.

Without taking a breath, Brother Lankford went on to the next miracle. There was a woman with part of her nose gone from cancer. He prayed for her, but nothing happened immediately. He told the lady that sometimes miracles don't happen instantly and to have faith. She came back the next night and her nose was perfect. Can you imagine?

Now it was finally Sister Lankford's turn again. A woman came from a foreign country by boat and then train to get to Azusa Street. She could hardly walk and couldn't speak any English. Her family accompanied her. Sister Lankford couldn't see anything wrong with her, but it was obvious that the woman was in pain.

"What is the matter with her?" she asked.

Her daughter said, "Feel her back." Sister Lankford felt a growth about the size of an arm all down the left side of her back.

Her daughter said, "It's very serious. It's black, and there's a split in it where stuff runs out. The doctor said she could die at any time."

Sister Lankford prayed over her. All of a sudden, the lady started gibbering something and jumping and running. Her family finally caught up with her and brought her back. "What was she saying?" Sister Lankford asked.

"She says it's healed." The daughter felt her mother's back. "My God, it's gone. It's gone!"

The Lankfords worked as a team on this next miracle. She told about the time four or five blind people were brought in from a home for the blind. Sister Lankford walked up to them and announced that God was going to work miracles. Brother Lankford ran over to them, covered their eyes and prayed for them, laying hands on each of them. Every time he removed his hands, the results were the same: they could see! Instant healings! The whole place erupted in shouting and dancing.

I asked if they remembered any specific miracles where God used Brother Seymour, and Sister Lankford's eyes lit up. "I recall witnessing two of the greatest miracles where Seymour was powerfully used by God."

I was all ears! First, she told about the man with the wooden leg. Seymour had approached a man with a wooden leg and asked, "What did you come here for?"

The man replied, "I want you to pray for my leg. It is starting to get gangrene where the wooden leg attaches."

Seymour replied, "I'm just upset because you have the wooden leg on. It would be a challenge for God to grow a leg out when the wooden leg is attached."

The man removed the wooden leg and stood before Seymour, balancing on his one good leg. Seymour laid hands on the man and proclaimed, "Let Thy Name be glorified. In the Name of Jesus, I command this leg to grow out. The gangrene is gone; you are healed."

Seymour didn't preach that night. The miracle spoke for itself. Rejoicing was continuous as the crowd went wild. The man ran upon the platform and around the room on *two* good legs! No one could get him to stop rejoicing and praising God.

Next Sister Lankford told of the man with no arm. He had lost his arm ten years earlier through a work-related accident. The arm had been totally severed at the shoulder.

Brother Seymour asked the crowd, "Would you like to see God have a wonderful time here tonight? Some of you may remember the man's leg that grew out about a year ago."

Seymour then asked the one-armed man, "Can you work with just the one arm?"

The man answered, "I'm just given minimal paying jobs, and I barely make enough money to even eat."

Seymour shook his head and responded, "That's not good. Are you married?"

"Yes."

"Got kids?"

"Yes."

Seymour declared, "This man needs to be able to make a living. This man needs to work, and he needs to be able to pay his tithe. Will you tithe if I pray for you and God gives you your arm back?" Seymour asked teasingly.

"Yes!" the man replied.

Seymour burst out laughing. "I'm just having fun."

He then slapped his hands on the shoulder itself and commanded the arm to grow out. Almost instantly it grew out! The healed man stood in total shock, then started moving his new arm and inspecting it with his other hand, wonderstruck by the miracle.

A few weeks later the man came back, bringing about 200 people with him, telling many at the meeting that he had gotten his old job back. Many of those he brought with him needed healing and left that evening fully restored as people in the crowd prayed and laid hands on each of them.

This last Lankford story is one of the most remarkable stories I ever heard from the saints. In 1908, a girl in her late teens, grossly scarred and ugly, was carried through the doors of Azusa on a cot. Her body was lathered in salve to soothe the excruciating pain of third degree burns that covered all of her. According to her family, all she wanted to do was die. But, they brought her down from Northern California to Azusa Street in the hope that she would be healed and live.

Sister Lankford saw her and came over to her. Her relatives told her that the girl was the victim of a devastating house fire. Sister Lankford looked at her and could actually see her bones in some areas where the flesh had been completely burned away. She lightly touched her and prayed for her. Then she covered her up with a blanket and said, "Let's see what God will do."

Every twenty minutes, she kept looking over at the girl. Sister Lankford could hardly contain herself because, little by little, there was more "meat" on the girl's body. It took not quite two hours and the teen was completely healed! They wiped the salve off of her body, and she got up off the cot. Her body was entirely made new.

The family stayed in town overnight and bought her some new clothes the next day. They returned to Azusa Street, and no one recognized the girl. They only recognized the family members. It was hard for even those at Azusa Street to believe this miracle. I wish I could have met her.

Time passed quickly at the Lankfords' home. The evening always ended too soon. As I would walk to my dorm room, my companions were the stories I'd re-live in my mind, marveling at the wondrous works that the Azusa Saints witnessed and participated in. I longed for the day that the Shekinah Glory would fall again—I wanted to be right in the middle of it. Heck, I even wanted to play in it like Riggs and Ward!

15

LET THE CHILDREN COME TO ME

Say Hello to Sister Dundee

~~~

AZUSA AGE: 22

I guess you could call Azusa a God party that lasted for more than three years. It was a constant celebration of the lavish love of the Father for His children. There was much to rejoice about, but nothing was more precious than the healing of His little children. I had the honor of knowing the saint, a young woman at that time, who understood and experienced such joy over and over as she sought out the little children whose sick or broken bodies needed God's touch.

Sister Dundee had been around Pisgah since the years of Dr. Yoakum. She even had a grandson, Teddy, who lived with Brother Smith and his family. While I was at Pisgah, she remarried. I often thought about her new husband's devotion to Sister Dundee and how they were such a beautiful, sweet couple. I also was kind of partial to him because he would take Teddy and me to eat breakfast at many of the better restaurants.

Sister Dundee was close to eighty years old when I met her. Her hair, black with a bit of gray, was pulled back into a glory bun. Italian by birth, Sister Dundee was a very quiet, sweet woman. She wore gold-rimmed glasses that hung or slid down to the end of her nose. Like Sister Carney, she wore those small granny boots with the hooks and eyelets. She was very healthy for her age and very well spoken.

She had experienced all kinds of miracles at Azusa, but I would have to coax and pull the stories out of her. At Azusa, she liked being around Sister Carney and adored Brother Anderson—relationships that continued at Pisgah. When I went to her home to hear her stories, her husband would sit on the floor right next to me, his face beaming. He was just as excited as I was because he couldn't get her to tell him those stories when they were by themselves.

Sister Dundee began her stories by telling about the crippled child on crutches, about seven or eight years old, brought to the meeting by her mother. The child had normal-sized legs but wore braces and needed crutches to walk. The little girl told Sister Dundee that she had been prayed for before, but nothing had happened. Sister Dundee sat down and talked to her and explained that if she got healed, it would bring great glory to Jesus. She told the child, "You are supposed to get healed at Azusa."

The little girl listened to her and said, "Okay. Pray for me."

Sister Dundee asked, "Has anyone ever taken your braces off before praying for you?"

"No."

Sister Dundee said, "Well, that needs to stop."

Together, they took the braces off while she was sitting down, and then Sister Dundee took the braces and crutches over to the other side of the room and came back to her. She gently smiled at the girl and said, "Now, you can't get those back because I won't bring them back to you. I will keep your mother busy so she can't get them for you. You're just going to have to get healed." Sister Dundee assured, "Darling, we've got to glorify Jesus. It would break His heart if you didn't get healed."

Tears welled up in the little girl's eyes as she almost started to cry. Sister Dundee told her, "All that is left for us to do is to start praying and obey Jesus, and you will be healed. Then Jesus will get the glory."

The little girl agreed, and Sister Dundee prayed for her. Within a few moments, the little girl said that she felt something in her feet—something she had never felt before! Sister Dundee told her to stand up and to start trying to move her feet. The little girl said, "I can't!"

Sister Dundee gently responded, "You need to try."

You could see the excitement rise as the little girl started moving her feet up and down. She looked down and started doing a dance like a little stomp. Then she started screaming that she was healed. Sister Dundee turned her loose, and she went dancing and stomping all over the warehouse, healed and whole.

Similarly, I remember Sister Dundee telling how she prayed for a young girl, maybe nine or ten, with one leg three to four inches shorter than the other. She could hardly walk, and she had one shoe with a really high sole. Sister Dundee saw her and said, "Come sit with me."

So the family came and sat with her. "Would you like for that short leg to grow out to be as long as the other one?"

"Yes. That's why we brought her to Azusa," the mother said.

"Good. Take her shoe off," said Sister Dundee.

She took the child's legs and held them. "I command you in the Name of Jesus to grow out." The leg gradually grew out in response to the command. The child couldn't walk that well at first. She wasn't used to that one leg hitting the ground that soon. She just took her time, and eventually, after about an hour, she could walk normally. Then she danced her thanksgiving to God.

Sister Dundee's next story was the most tender of all her Azusa stories. As far as she was concerned, the younger the child, the better she liked it. There was a child not yet a year old with a bow in the neck. The baby would not cry or make any noise, but the mother said that she could tell that the baby was in pain. Sister Dundee asked the mother if she could pray for her baby. When the mother agreed, she took the child from her, putting the baby blanket over its head so that the mother couldn't see.

She prayed for the baby, and she tried not to get too excited because she was holding the baby in her arms. She had to contain herself when the bow started to disappear. She told me that she had to make sure not to throw a "Pentecostal fit."

When the bow straightened out, Sister Dundee just stood there crying as the baby looked up at her and smiled. Finally, she heard the mother ask what was happening. "Why are you crying? Is there something wrong with my baby?"

Sister Dundee stood there, loving on the child as she pulled the blanket back and showed the smiling, healed baby to her.

I asked, "Did you give the baby back to its mother?"

Sister Dundee said, "Oh, Lord, no, I couldn't have caught that mother if I had wanted to. The mother just went running around rejoicing!"

I asked about the father, and she said that the father wasn't at the meeting, but Sister Dundee met him later. The mother took the baby back home and showed the father his healed baby. Not only did he come to the revival after that, but he also got saved and became the pastor of one of the larger churches in the Los Angeles area for about thirty-five-plus years.

Sister Dundee also told of a little boy who had to have his head and his body strapped into his wheelchair to hold him up. She went over to the boy and asked his parents, "What is wrong with him?"

The parents were not exactly sure. He had some kind of paralysis but could breathe on his own. She told them, "Well, this is good, for the Lord's Name will be glorified, but we can't just pray for him and leave him tied up here." Sister Dundee started undoing the strap on his neck and told his parents to hold his body up.

After she got everything loosened, she laid her hands on him and cried out, "In the Name of Jesus Christ, be made perfectly whole." Sister Dundee said that immediately the boy jerked and then wanted to get down to play.

I asked, "Well, how old was he?"

Sister Dundee said, "Maybe he was six."

I said, "You mean a little bitty kid?"

Sister Dundee just smiled and said, "Yes, a little bitty kid. I had barely gotten out the words 'In the Name of Jesus,' and he was healed."

Sister Dundee told me that she got to see this boy many times over the next three years during the revival and about a year after that. The little boy affectionately called Sister Dundee "Mammy" from the time of his healing up until the last time she saw him.

Now, scarlet fever was a plague back at the turn of last century. In the worst of cases, an entire family of children could be wiped out in a week or two. Think of that!

One day Sister Dundee found a little girl who was left spastic from scarlet fever. She was in a wheelchair, jerking and spasming.

Sister Dundee walked up to her and said, "Hi."

Her family said, "She doesn't know what you're saying."

"I'm getting her in practice," Sister Dundee said, "because before long, she's going to know exactly what I said. Do I have permission from you to lay hands on her?"

They said, "Well, yes."

So she laid hands on her and prayed, but not before she put up the foot flaps. It wasn't faith if you didn't put up the flaps according to the Carney Rule. They're going to get up out of that wheelchair!

She put the flaps up and prayed for this little girl. It wasn't an instantaneous healing—it took maybe about three minutes for this girl to quit the jerking.

"What is your name?" Sister Dundee asked. The girl answered her. "Would you like to get up and go back there with the other young people to play?"

"Yes!"

The little girl jumped up and ran to the back with the other kids. Of course, the mama and daddy and Sister Dundee had a dancing good time. I think I would have, too, if I had an ill child healed in three minutes and off playing with the other kids.

The following miracle took healing to a brand-new level for me. I guarantee you, ask anybody today, and they'd all agree that Down syndrome or Mongoloidism can't be healed. But Sister Dundee would tell you differently if she were here. She prayed for maybe two dozen of those who were healed from this disorder, and I was lucky enough to meet one of them.

I don't remember his name, but he was a little old man by the time I met him. His face had all the characteristics of someone who has Down syndrome, but he acted completely normal. After God touched him through the prayers of Sister Dundee, he grew up and became a professor of music and taught in a California university.

Sister Dundee remembered the day he was healed. He looked at her and said, "You're not Jesus."

She smiled and said to the mother, "Explain to him that he's fine now." Of course, the mother couldn't talk. She was shaking her head in disbelief and crying. Her son was just healed of Down syndrome!

This next story surprised me even more. I still marvel when I think of it. One day Sister Dundee found a horribly disfigured child around five years old amongst the people at Azusa Street. He had scars all around on his head.

His family said that doctors literally had to piece his face back together after he fell from a staircase onto a concrete floor when he was about two-and-a-half years old. The side of his face that took the impact was about one-quarter of an inch lower than the rest of his head.

Sister Dundee could tell he wasn't normal mentally either. Her reaction? "Oh, how marvelous! God gets glory when things like this happen."

The father asked, "Things like what?"

"He's going to be healed," she declared.

See, by this time, they didn't say "God will." They said, "He is healed." They had so much confidence that God was going to heal everyone and everything. "Let me hold the boy in my lap," she said as she set him down and laid her hand on his head.

Sister Dundee said she could see and feel her hand moving and shifting as she was praying. Finally she took her hand away, and the boy's face was perfectly normal! He was healed mentally as well.

Now, here's the shocker. This disfigured child grew up to be a handsome Hollywood star. His name was Robert Montgomery. He became an actor, on stage and screen, as well as a director.

In 1937, he was nominated for an Academy Award for Best Actor for a thriller called *Night Must Fall*. His daughter, Elizabeth Montgomery, starred in the hit TV show *Bewitched* in the 1960s.

From grotesque disfigurement to a golden boy in Hollywood. How's that for a miracle?

Sister Dundee was part of Azusa almost the entire time the revival lasted. She, too, loved the Shekinah Glory and the music that seemed to fall from heaven. She loved it all, but nothing compared to the love she felt and expressed for the children in need of their Father's touch.

16

THE STORY THAT IS TRUE FROM UNDER THE PEW

Say Hello to Phyllis

❦

Azusa Age: 3

I'm here to set the record straight on this story. Mistakenly, the identity of this child was attributed to Jean Darnall in my previous book. This is not the truth. Here's the real story behind this tiny toddler of three and Pastor Darnall.

On a night in 1963, there was going to be a meeting with three speakers at Angeles Temple. One of them was Pastor Jean Darnall, who had taken over the pastorship of Angeles Temple after Aimee Semple McPherson in 1944. I went to hear her speak.

Pastor Jean would often visit Pisgah to speak, and she liked to spend time with the young people there, including me. We had come to know one another. Pastor Darnall's quiet and gentle spirit made everyone who met her feel comfortable and loved.

She stood about 5'4" to my 6'2", but I will never forget what it was like to have her lay her hands on my head and pray for me. The power of God flowed through her tender touch.

Once when I asked her why she chose to spend time with my friend, Mike, and me, she said, "You two men are very young, but you know what you are doing, and you know God!" So, I came to hear my friend's message this night.

As usual, I arrived at the service early. A lady came up to me and sat down next to me. "Are you Brother Tommy?" she asked.

I said, "Yes."

"The one the Azusa Street saints tell their stories to?"

"Yes." Then she asked if she could tell me the story of her aunt who was at Azusa Street.

Her aunt, whose name was Phyllis, came to Azusa Street late in 1909, a couple of months before the ending of the Shekinah Glory. Phyllis was just about three years old. She could remember being under the pews, ready to take a nap but not tired enough to be unaware of this "misty stuff" that was all around her.

Phyllis tried to gather it in her arms and poke some of it down the pockets of her dress, but she couldn't do it. She remembered watching people and seeing these marvelous healings happening all around her. She remembered the dancing, shouting and rejoicing.

She was too young to fully understand, but later on she came to realize the moves of God she witnessed from under the pew. Phyllis would re-live it time and time again to her niece. Thankfully, her niece shared these memories with me.

The only connection between Pastor Darnall and Phyllis is that I came to know Phyllis' story while waiting to hear Pastor Darnall speak. To honor Phyllis, her niece, and Pastor Darnall, this is the real story that is now setting the record straight.

17

AFTER AZUSA: MIRACLES AT PISGAH

*"Then Moses went up to Mount Nebo from the plains
of Moab and climbed Pisgah Peak....Then the LORD
said to Moses, 'This is the land I promised on oath
to Abraham, Isaac, and Jacob....'"* (Deuteronomy 34:1,4)

❦

*God showed Moses the land He promised to the father of our faith
from Pisgah Peak. Pisgah Home, the community in which Tommy lived
with the Azusa Street saints, was named after this biblical mountain.
Pisgah Home was founded in 1895 as a place of hope and the promise of
new beginnings by its founder, Dr. Yoakum. But Pisgah's indirect incep-
tion began in 1894.*

*While on his way to a Methodist church-related meeting in July of
1894, a drunken buggy driver collided with Dr. Yoakum. A piece of
metal protruding from the buggy pierced Dr. Yoakum's back, broke several ribs and caused internal hemorrhaging. A medical exam revealed the
injuries should have been fatal. An infection soon set in and lasted for
several months.*

In pursuit of relief from his sufferings, Dr. Yoakum moved from Texas to the milder climate of Los Angeles. This helped, but not enough. Almost desperate, Dr. Yoakum visited Christian Alliance Church on Figueroa Street in Highland Park. The pastor, W.C. Stevens, prayed for him. A spontaneous miracle took place, and he was instantly healed. His life's calling was permanently changed.

Abandoning his medical practice as a brain surgeon in which he made $18,000 a month at the turn of the last century, he dedicated the rest of his life to serving the chronically ill, the poor and destitute, and the social outcasts. In February of 1895, he opened up Pisgah Home in Highland Park to fulfill the divine direction he had been given to create a mission for the needy. He gave his workers pockets full of nickels and instructed them to go to skid row in downtown Los Angeles. The workers would minister to the down and out and pick people up from the streets. They would ride the streetcar for a nickel each to Avenue 60, then walk one block to Pisgah where those in need would live, rehabilitatem and become a part of the community.

This skid-row ministry was still going strong when Tommy arrived in 1960, brought there by Sister Goldie. Tommy recalls, "The first time I came [to Pisgah], there was like a curtain hanging around that place. There was such peace."

Years earlier, in 1906 and 1907, Pisgah hosted many followers of the Azusa Street Revival. As you've read, many of the saints, who were young at that time, came to live in this community when they were elderly to fellowship with one another and serve others who also called Pisgah their home.

Reverend Harold James Smith, who took over the pastorship of Pisgah in 1950, had a vision for revival, making Pisgah the perfect setting for the saints to continue working the gifts of the Holy Spirit—just as they did at Azusa Street.

❧

From 1960 to 1966, Tommy listened to stories of miracles from Azusa Street. At Pisgah, he was able to witness the miracles. Tommy recalls…

Sister Dundee at Pisgah...

I remember how Sister Dundee told stories of healing children at Azusa. She continued healing children at Pisgah. In fact, the families that came to Pisgah for church services didn't have very many medical bills. They'd bring their kids to those saints, the saints would pray for them and the children would be healed. Now, Sister Dundee sought out babies. She'd heal anyone, but she had a heart for the infants.

One day a woman brought this baby, wrapped in his swaddling clothes, that had this tumor like a black knot on the side of its head. It looked pretty serious. Naturally, everyone went looking for Sister Dundee.

They found her, and she came to the mother and baby. "Oh, how wonderful, darling," she said to the baby. She reached over and kissed it right on the tumor. She lay the blanket over it and prayed for a few seconds, then walked away, saying, "Wait for maybe ten minutes and then remove the blanket."

Sister Dundee waddled into the church with her happy little husband by her side. I followed them into church and sat down. Suddenly, I heard this bloodcurdling scream and went to find out what was happening. I saw the father taking the baby from the mother because the mother was going hysterical, screaming so loud you could hear her a block away.

When the mother removed the blanket, there was nothing there— the tumor was gone! I said to the father, "I want to see the baby."

He showed me the child, and I said, "Look at that, man! Why don't you give me the baby and you go do a happy dance?"

He said, "Thanks, Tommy, but I just want to admire my child."

The miracle I remember most with Sister Dundee at Pisgah was this desperate couple who came all the way from England with their dying baby. The little one was only twelve or fourteen months old and had leukemia. It didn't have much longer to live and seemed unconscious.

They flew to the States, came to Pisgah and found Sister Dundee before church service. She walked over to the baby in their arms, prayed for it and walked away into church, almost like she was confidently leaving the rest up to God.

The baby finally came to, and before the service was through, the baby was in the nursery. The parents just went crazy with joy.

Brother Brown at Pisgah...

Unfortunately, old Brother Bill Brown didn't have much joy, if any. I called him the sad sack because he'd sit around Pisgah at times, tears coming down his face. As I mentioned before, he mourned the loss of the Shekinah Glory.

God still honored this sweet, broken vessel by continuing to heal through him. Bill continued to pray for blind people. One day there was this little old lady who was stone blind. Brother Bill came up to her. "God said to come over and pray for you, so I'm going to pray for you."

She said, "Oh, pray for someone else." She had been blind since she was in her mid-thirties, and now she was a very old woman.

Bill said, "Don't tell me not to obey God." So he took "grandma's" big, thick, black glasses off and took her cane and broke it. Everybody thought, "Oh, Jesus, now she has to get healed."

He laid his hands on her face and covered her eyes. He prayed for her and then took his hands away. She could see!

There were probably about fifty people in a circle around her. They all had a shouting good time because grandma's eyes were completely healed. Completely.

Mother Mangrum, Brother Anderson and Sister Lucille at Pisgah...

Now, people weren't the only ones healed at Pisgah. I saw those saints heal beloved animals as well. We had lots of cats around. One day there was a cat with its eye shot out. The cat was brought to Mother Mangrum.

She laid hands on the cat's eye, prayed for it, and when she took her hand away, the eyeball was back! It was gone and then back.

We also had a dog at Pisgah named Patty. She belonged to Reverend Smith and his family. I called her a Pentecostal dog. The first night I was there at Pisgah, I sat right by the door during the church service. I didn't know what these people were going to do, so I sat by the door in order to dash if I wanted to.

Mrs. Smith, we called her Mother Smith, and the twelve-year-old Smith twins were sitting not too far away. They didn't have air conditioning back then, so in the summertime they left the door standing open. Patty, the dog, crawled in and got under my seat.

Since this was my first time in the service, I didn't know that when Brother Smith got excited, he'd pick up a tambourine and start banging it and singing and dancing. Well, he got excited that night, and Patty let out this "roar." I leaped in the air and ran out of the church. Remember, I was sitting right on top of her.

The Smith twins ran out and caught me and told me that was just their dog. "You sure? It sounded like a devil to me!" I said. They told me that Patty always roars when their father sings and dances with the tambourine.

In 1961, Patty got sick. Her left hip was inflamed, and the doctor said it was extremely painful. She couldn't stand on it. Patty looked pitiful, and the twins were really distraught.

I prayed for her, but she didn't get healed. That hurt me because Patty and I were good friends at this point. Brother Anderson came to Patty and started talking to her. Then he prayed for her, and she was instantly healed. She got up and started jumping around and playing right then and there.

"Does God love you more than me?" I asked him.

He said, "What's the matter, Brother Tommy?"

"I prayed for her, and she didn't get healed."

Kindly, he said, "Well, she knows me more than she knows you."

I have to admit, I was jealous, that his prayers worked and mine didn't.

Right across the street from Pisgah, there was this little boy who had befriended Sister Lucille. He had a big boxer bulldog named Tubby. That dog was as ugly as homemade soap, but I loved him as much as that little boy. Tubby was playful.

One day, about a block away on Avenue 60, Tubby got hit by a car. The little boy came running to find Sister Lucille. He grabbed her by the hand and started dragging her. "Well, now, stop pulling. We'll get there," Sister Lucille said.

"What if he dies?" the little guy complained.

"We'll raise him from the dead, but stop pulling me."

I followed them because I wanted to see for myself what was going to happen. We got to the scene of the accident, and there was blood and gore. I said to myself, "All right. I've got to see this."

Sister Lucille said to everyone gathered around, "If you would all get back, let me pray for him."

The police officer said and kept saying, "Ma'am, the dog is dead." I looked closely, and I couldn't see the dog breathing.

"That's my dog and you get back!" the little boy said.

That officer looked at that desperate little guy. "All right, young man."

Lucille knelt beside Tubby and prayed, "God, this little boy loves this dog. He dragged me all the way down here. Now, I want You to perform a miracle to impress on this little boy's heart that You love this dog, too. I command you, Tubby, to be healed in Jesus' Name."

All of a sudden, dust flew out from Tubby's nose. All bloody, he got up and came over to us. That little boy swooped Tubby up and just started playing with that bloody, beloved dog.

This was in 1961. Tubby was still alive when I left in '66.

TOMMY AT PISGAH...

When I first got to Pisgah in 1960, I was only seventeen years old. I was just a kid living among these saints! If I wasn't talking with them, we were eating together three times a day. We had prayer from 11 o'clock to 12 noon every day and church service every night.

In church, I'd watch them. If I saw one of them jerk his or her head, I'd jerk my head. I wasn't mocking them. I was mimicking them. I was doing what they did because I wanted what they had. Did it work? Yes.

All of a sudden, the power of God would hit me, and I'd really get a blessing. Often they'd lay their hands on my shoulders and bow their heads, and I'd see their lips mouthing a five- or six-second prayer. I finally asked, "What are y'all doing when you do that?"

Brother Sines said, "We're imputing all the anointings that we have onto you."

I said, "Oh, okay."

I couldn't wait to get to my little section in the men's dormitory and get out Mr. Webster's book to find out what in the world *impute* meant. It means the same thing as transfer over. I thought, "Wow, I'm getting all their anointings. Wow, okay." It would take a bit of growing up for me to understand the significance of what they were doing.

As I received their anointings, it became clear that I also needed to be healed. I may have been only seventeen years old, but I was already a heavy smoker and a drinker. My daddy was a moonshiner. He made and distributed corn liquor and thought it was funny to slip some of it to me in my bottle when I was just a toddler. I even grew up eating watermelons that had been injected with wine or hard liquor and left for a few days for the meat of the melon to marinate. And boy, did I smoke.

It was the second day that I was at Pisgah when I was down to my last cigarette. I knew I was in trouble because I wanted one but had no money. I smoked thirty cigarettes a day and one cigar. I smoked twenty Pall Malls, ten Lucky Strikes, and one five-cent cigar, or a Rum Crook.

"Brother Cantrell, I've got a nicotine habit," I said. "I need deliverance, and I need it bad." He didn't say a word. He only smiled.

I had nice hair, but he slapped his hand on top of my pretty 'do and prayed for me. Man, I didn't feel anything, so I'm thinking, "Well, he didn't have the Holy Ghost. That didn't work."

I had to go across the street to the railroad tracks because there was no smoking on the church grounds. The tracks were called Tobacco Road because that is where you could smoke. I took out my last Pall Mall, lit it up and took a big drag.

I almost choked to death! I stood there, confused. I took another big drag on it, and I wound up throwing up! I put the Pall Mall in my shirt pocket, walked back across the street to Pisgah and went upstairs to bed, feeling sick, but thinking that I would need this cigarette in the morning, anticipating a nicotine fit. I had a bad habit.

Now, Pisgah had intercoms all over the place, and at 7:15 in the morning, the Herald of Hope broadcast came on, which was a message by Pastor Smith, waking up all eighty-seven people who lived on the grounds. At 7:15, I sat up and froze in bed. I didn't want to smoke! I haven't smoked since. It's been fifty-two years.

In August of 1960, I went to Brother Cantrell and told him that I had another problem. I loved the smell of bars. I would walk past them and fight the urge to go inside.

Brother Cantrell smiled and slapped hands on my head, messing up my 'do again. I never saw him do that to anyone else, so I think he was trying to humble me. He prayed, "God, every time Tommy comes by a bar, he is to get nauseous. He'll have to run to get away from it or throw up." He finished, "In Jesus' Name."

Again, I didn't feel anything when he prayed for me. I like to get the "Jesus bumps," but I never felt a tingle or a touch of the Holy Spirit. That didn't matter. Something happened whether I felt anything or not. Fifty-two years later, I can't get close to a bar.

About a month after I received the Baptism, they wanted me to go down to skid row and testify. That idea scared the tooties out of this simple, country boy. I was shy back then, afraid of what people would think. What if I said something dumb? Quite often, that's exactly what I did.

"Brother Cantrell, they want me to go down to skid row and…"

"I know," he said. "I'm the one who suggested they take you."

I said, "Well, I need you to pray for me. I need a holy boldness."

Again he laid hands on me. Before we left, I had to go to the bathroom to re-comb my hair.

We went down to skid row, and, to my amazement, they couldn't shut me up on the way down or when we were there. There was about eight of those bums—we called them bums back then—who came to the Lord because of my testimony.

Pastor Smith said, "It's hard to believe you were ever shy." Marlene, my wife, doesn't believe I ever was shy. I can be in front of a few people or thousands. I haven't had a problem with shyness since that day I asked for holy boldness.

Needless to say, if I got a sniffle, I didn't run and get a cold tablet. I ran to Brother Cantrell. "Brother Cantrell, I'm getting a cold. Pray for me."

He'd say, "All right."

Every time, I got healed. Little did I know that God was also going to use me to heal.

While I lived at Pisgah, I visited heaven three times after I was saved. The first time I was at a Katherine Kuhlman meeting; the second time I was on vacation in a tiny town in Texas at a Pentecostal church where my mother attended. The last time I was at Pisgah, during Sunday service, in 1963.

There was nothing special about the day, and I didn't feel any differently. Brother Smith said, "Well, it's 11 o'clock. Let's get up and worship the Lord." I stood up and stuck my hands up in the air, and I went into my third and last vision of heaven.

> *Each visit, I sit on this grassy knoll. This time, I'm rolling on it. The grass makes a sound, like a cat purring. I'm almost petting the grass, it feels so good. Everything is alive in heaven!*

There are dogs, cats and horses there. I look around and see the same big, beautiful flowers that look like tulips that else seen in my other two visions. I can't describe their color—it's like nothing I've ever seen before. The first and second time, the flowers turned toward me as if they were looking at me. This time, I say, "Hey, guys!" They start to shake as if they are saying hi, too.

I look around, and I see these people come by wearing beautiful robes just as before. I shout, "Glory!" I can hear thunderous "glory!" echo all over.

Heaven is a lot like earth, only bigger. Everything is so clear! And there is the presence of perfect peace.

When I came out of that vision, I took my hands down. My hands weren't hurting. I looked around the church, and all the ladies had cried their makeup all over their faces. People were slain in the Spirit.

I looked at the young people, and they were all crying. I looked at Sister Smith, Brother Smith's wife. She's sitting there, tears just pouring out of her eyes. I'm thinking, "What's the matter with her? What's going on?"

"Sister Smith, what time is it?"

She looked. "It's about three minutes after one," and then she smiled sweetly at me and winked. That wasn't like Sister Smith to wink. I couldn't believe it. It had just been 11 o'clock.

I knew that I had been in my vision for a while. I thought thirty minutes. It was two hours later! I look over at Brother Sines and Brother Christopher, crying like babies.

I thought, "What's happened? What's gone on?"

"Tommy, I kept looking at your eyes. Your eyelids never even blinked," my friend, Vivian, told me. "Your mouth was kind of gapped open a little bit, but it didn't even look like you were breathing. You looked like a statue."

I found out that the Shekinah Glory had fallen all around me. I didn't move or even bat an eyelash for two hours. Brother Smith, with tears coming down his face, smiled at me and finally said, "We don't need a sermon today. We've had church." Everybody said, "Yeah, amen." After that people treated me with a lot more respect for some reason.

People all over heard about this, and I got invitations from all over the country.

Big-time ministers came by because they had to meet Tommy. I was called "Pisgah's teenage fireball of Pentecost."

I started to pray for people and heal them, but I had to get used to the idea. In the Sunday school room, one of the young girls, Cheryl Meyers, had migraine headaches. She was starting to cry one day, and Glenda Soda kept glaring at me.

Finally I said, "What?"

She said, "Get up and heal her."

I walked over to her and said, "Cheryl, I'm going to lay hands on you. Where does it hurt?"

"Right in here," she said, indicating the side of her head. Tears were pouring down her cheeks.

I said, "Okay."

I gently laid my hand on her and started praying. She reached up and slapped her hand on my head and said, "Don't stop praying!" Well, I didn't stop. I kept on praying, then I went into tongues. Finally she was just sitting there smiling…and healed.

One day God told me to pray for Cheryl's father. I heard God say, "Go pray for Brother Meyers." I walked up to him and laid hands on him and prayed. He jerked and looked back at me. I prayed for him again, and he jerked again. I didn't know why I was praying. God just said to go and pray. I found out later that God used me to heal him of colon cancer.

Remember how Brother Cantrell prayed for me to trade in my shyness for holy boldness? Well, I took that boldness to a park near Pisgah that had been taken over by teenyboppers and a gang of drug dealers. They didn't want any kids under ten or over thirteen. Some older people got killed because they just happened to be there. When the sun went down, these bad seeds ruled.

Well, Preacher Tommy, as they called me, would go down there and talk to them. The young girls liked me because when they would sit down by me, I wouldn't touch them in improper places. They knew I was the real thing.

I would pray for them and tell them to go down to the mission, and Brother Johnny, Frank Bartleman's son and the Pisgah main cook, would give them ice cream. I'd tell Johnny, "If they come down for ice cream, you get them to come to church." He and I were working together.

This made me a target for the gangs. "Preacher Tom, we're gonna kill you, man. Leave the kids alone," they warned.

I said, "Why? So you can kill them with drugs? No!"

They threatened again, "We're gonna kill you."

I said, "That's up to God."

One afternoon they caught me on the Avenue 60 bridge in Pasadena.

I was witnessing to a boy named Henry who came looking for the crazy hillbilly he had heard about named Tommy. At this point, I was 6'2", 200 pounds with a 32" waist and biceps that bulged without flexing. Henry was built, too, but only 5'8".

He and I were crossing the bridge when this gang pulled up in a car behind us. "We're gonna kill you, Preacher Tom," they said while getting out of the car. We stopped and turned around. Both of us had our shirts off because it was a hot, summer day.

Now, there were six of them and only the two of us. They looked at us and got back in the car and drove away. A short while later, they came back with weapons. One of them hit me in the ribs with a piece of reinforced iron. Another kid hit me in the face with the leg of an antique chair that was like a big, thick club. It broke my glasses and my nose. I went down, but it never really knocked me out. They kicked and hit me while I was on the ground. Henry stopped a car that was passing by and got me back to Pisgah.

I don't really remember much. I recall hearing, "He was such a dynamic Christian, a young…." Another voice said, "Shut up! He still *is*, not was." Then the lights went out.

I'm told I fell forward, face down. They took me to Los Angeles General Hospital and had me examined. The nurse asked what had happened to me. I told her.

"That blow to your ribs should have killed you. Your ribs should have been crushed, but they're not even broken. Your face should have been caved in, but your nose is just a little broken. It's not that serious."

I asked, "What about these bruises around my eyes?"

She said, "They'll all heal. They're not that bad. You're in extremely good shape," she said. "That's what saved you."

I didn't argue with her. I thought, "No, God saved me."

"Are you going to go back to that park?" she asked.

I said, "Absolutely. As soon as I can walk normally, I'm going to go back down there." I wasn't going to let the devil win that battle.

That drug ring was finally disbanded. The kids turned them in, and churches in the area were flooded with the park teenyboppers. About 120 of them came to church with me. Victory!

In Matthew 10:8, Jesus said to heal the sick, cast out demons and raise the dead. I had covered two of those three bases, until about a month after I was bathed in the Shekinah Glory. During a church service, Brother Silver, a retired attorney, screamed, grabbed at his heart and fell back over the pew. Dr. Dodge, who was also in the service, ran over to him. He checked him twice. "He's dead," the doctor pronounced.

Sister Smith yelled to Peggy Johnson who was just walking by, "Go and get Tommy Welchel." She had to say my last name because there were many Tommys around Pisgah. "Go now, Peggy!"

Peggy found me. "Sister Smith said to come to the church. Now!" Peggy was so firm, I didn't question. I went.

"Look at Brother Silver over there," Sister Smith told me.

I looked at him and said, "He looks dead to me."

She said, "Go raise him."

I said, "What? Huh?"

"I said, go raise him," she repeated.

"You want me to go over there and raise him from the dead?"

"Yes. Now," she said.

I slowly started walking to Brother Silver. I stopped. "Tommy, go raise him!" Sister Smith commanded me. I mean, come on. Raise the dead? "I've seen you pray for people and heal them. I've seen you cast out devils," she said. "I've never seen you raise the dead."

Now I'm scared. I wanted to ask, "Why me?"

"Thomas, raise him!" she demanded. How dare she call me by my real name! Now I'm mad.

I threw my left leg across Brother Silver. I laid my left hand on his chest, my right hand on his head, and I screamed loudly, "I command you to come back to earth from the dead now in Jesus' Name!"

Suddenly, I felt something like electricity shoot out of my hands. It bounced him. He shuddered and looked up at me. I looked down at him. He was viciously angry. That man was mad!

He got up, and his nose was so close to mine that if we both puckered, we would have kissed. "I was in heaven!" he said.

Finally I said, "She made me do it!" pointing to Sister Smith.

They all burst into laughter but Brother Silver and me. I slowly got off of him. I kept my hands out in front of me to make sure he didn't sock me. Then I got out of there. Brother Silver was to live another five years.

Of course, after that, I was in demand to go speak at different places. And who paid my way? Brother Silver did.

I left California to go to Georgia in 1968. I had been gone from Pisgah for two years. Brother Silver was dying, and he told everyone that he wanted to go home. One day he found my friend, who still lived there, and grabbed him by the shirt collar along with some chest hair. "I'm gonna die. Don't you tell Tommy Welchel *anything* until after I'm buried."

Once they buried him, my friend called and told me. I started laughing. I don't blame Brother Silver. I didn't want to leave heaven either.

18

MODERN-DAY MANNA: MIRACLES OF TODAY

"Those who believed what Peter said were baptized and added to the church that day—about 3,000 in all. A deep sense of awe came over them all, and the apostles performed many miraculous signs and wonders." (Acts 2:41,43)

Revival means to revive or restore back to life or consciousness. Sometimes a pastor or minister wants to "wake up" his or her congregation or even grow its numbers. An evangelist will come and infuse fresh ideas into the minds of the congregants to spiritually spark them back to life and to a new level of spiritual awareness. A revival is really for the saints, the believers. To be revived, there has to be something—faith—revivable.

⁓

The Azusa Street Revival is really a misnomer. Azusa Street was an awakening! As in the Upper Room in the Book of Acts, it first shook its own, then eventually the whole world. Not just Christians. Everybody. An awakening is for all, not just for the saints.

Azusa Street wasn't planned. It was prayed down. There is a "physicality," if you will, to the realm of the Spirit. Revelation 5:8 speaks of this: "…and they held gold bowls filled with incense, which are the prayers of God's people." I like the way Tommy puts it: "Rain doesn't fall. Rain never falls. It keeps collecting and getting so heavy that gravity pulls it down."

The power of God works the same way. We keep praying and praying until the bowls get so heavy with prayers, we pull heaven down. That's what they did at Azusa Street. That's what Bartleman was doing with his prayer groups all over the city prior to the outpouring.

"I'm going to keep telling people these stories from Azusa" Tommy says, "until the prayers of God's people get so heavy, we pull it down again." According to Tommy, "We don't have to contend to have the hundred-year prophecy fulfilled, but we have a part to play. That role is mainly praying and seeking God, and to keep on seeking that anointing until we pull it down. Remember, it's just like rain."

Don't forget, we are living in the period of the prophecy! This time it's going to be bigger, better and global. The prophecy is now coming to pass in different parts of the world. People are hungry for this next outpouring. The release of Tommy's first book was a trigger for this anticipated, mightier move of God, as we are about to show.

It makes me wonder—were we the holy envy of Parham, Seymour, and all the people of Azusa Street when they were still alive?

❧

So many people get excited and want to talk to me about the hundred-year prophecy. "Have you seen any of it?" they ask. I say, "You bet I have!" I get calls from all over the world.

One of my favorite testimonies is from a missionary to China named Brother X. He's asked me not to give his real name because his life would be in danger if his identity was known. He and other missionaries print my first book in Malaysia for $.27 a copy. Then they smuggle the books into the country and give them away for free.

I called Brother X and asked, "Brother, how many books have you gotten into China?"

He said, "Over 200,000."

"Wow!"

He said, "Brother Tommy, they don't know any better than to believe. They are having the same thing they had at Azusa Street. Even the Chinese soldiers go by, and they see glory over there [places where meetings are held]. They don't go in. They're scared."

I asked, "How often do miracles happen?"

He said, "Miracles happen at all their meetings. They're having limbs grow out. They're raising the dead. They're having it all in China now."

I said, "That's great! How about salvations?"

Brother X said, "We figure an average of three per book."

I said, "Over 600,000 people?"

He said, "That's right, Brother Tommy. All of China is having revival. They just keep it quiet."

He finished by saying, "There's only one book that's more popular than your book in China—the Bible."

Jumping across a couple of oceans to South America, an American missionary named Brother Paul Borel found my book and read it. Fluent in Portuguese, he went to an open-air church gathering of 9,300 people in Brazil. Brother Paul didn't know that they had been praying to see this kind of manifestation. He just stood up and started reading from my book.

When he read about the Shekinah Glory, people started falling out in the Spirit. I asked about how many fell out. "All of them," he said. "Nine thousand, three hundred people were slain in the Spirit." I couldn't believe it. He said, "You couldn't walk down the aisles. There were people everywhere."

I asked him what he and the pastors did during this time. "We waited for them all to come to." I can just imagine that scene. All those people. I love that testimony.

Closer to home, my book was read by Todd Bentley of the Lakeland Revival. I was interviewed by Sid Roth, and Sid said to me, "Tommy, Todd Bentley talks and sounds like he must have read your book." I told Sid that I knew he had.

Todd had thirty-one resurrections during his time at Lakeland. Some of the people he raised weren't even there. Family members called on the phone, Todd prayed and the deceased revived. Now, that's revival! Todd didn't even have to lay hands on people for the healings or resurrections.

See, you don't have to be in church, and you don't have to have hands laid on you.

I was at a church this one time, a pretty good-sized church in the San Fernando Valley in California, and we had a revival break out where many people got healed.

Many of them got up out of their seats and were healed just by watching other people whom I was praying over get healed. I was in a hurry to get on down to Coronado Island by San Diego, and I said, "Everybody who needs to be healed, reach your hands up here toward me."

I prayed a mass prayer, and as we were leaving, people kept coming up to me with healing testimonies. That thrilled me! This one little old black lady said she had arthritis so bad she had to wear diapers because she couldn't get to the bathroom in time. Now I'm watching her prance around, and she said, "Look at me, Brother Tommy!"

I asked, "So when I said that mass prayer, you got healed?"

She said, "Yes, I got healed."

Hands-off healing, so to speak, is one of my favorite things to see happen. Only a few times have I laid hands on people. See, I'm not the healer. The Holy Spirit is. Those who are healed are receiving from God the healing that happened 2,000 years ago on the cross. Many times I'll be speaking about the miracles at Azusa and that same healing will take place in the audience.

One of my favorite examples of this happened here in the States, outside Albany, New York, in the spring of 2012. I was invited by a Messianic rabbi to a conference. I'm up at the front telling my stories, and I was talking about Sister Lucille and the fun she had with teeth growing out.

All of a sudden, I heard this "Oooh!" from a lady in the back of the room.

I said, "Is something wrong back there, sister?"

The other woman sitting beside her said, "No, Brother Tommy. She just had a tooth grow in where one was missing!" Now, I didn't lay hands on her. I didn't even pray for a tooth. Just telling the story released the miracle.

In October of 2012, I had another hands-free healing at a speaking engagement in Tyler, Texas. I was praying a prayer of impartation for this sixteen-year-old girl. As I prayed, I noticed that she started to cry. I thought that the Holy Spirit was touching her as she received the anointing.

A little while later, the girl came up to me accompanied by her mother. I found out the reason she was crying. Since birth, she had been totally deaf in her left ear. While I was praying the prayer of impartation, the deaf ear popped open, and she was able to hear perfectly in that ear for the first time in her life. Those were tears of sheer joy. It tickled me that a healing was received for something I didn't even know about, let alone pray for. Just goes to show you—I'm not the one who is doing the healing.

My friend, Brother Steve Siler, based in Moore, Oklahoma, has an astounding tooth ministry. There have been over 2,000 miracles in people's mouths in the way of gold and silver fillings, enamel fillings, even new teeth altogether! I've been at some of his meetings to witness this phenomena.

I remember this one night, a woman received a gold filling in a rotten tooth. I looked inside her mouth and saw something glitter other than the gold. We got a magnifying glass and inspected the sparkle. Sure enough, there was a diamond in the middle of the gold as if set by a jeweler. Steve told me at one event, a pastor's wife received four diamonds in her teeth. At another gathering, Steve said a sixty-six-year-old woman received eight gold teeth. She went to her dentist, and three professionals in that office confirmed the gold was 23 karat, finer than 24 karat gold!

Brother Steve travels all over the country. He has even led crusades in conjunction with Sid Roth. Steve has taken my first book and read it out loud at his gatherings. "Every time I take Tommy's book to a meeting, an atmosphere of expectation is created, which becomes a breeding ground for miracles," Steve says. "A landslide of the miraculous" occurs when he reads from it.

Showers of gold have rained down and glory clouds have appeared. I've seen it when I've attended his meetings. I remember this one time, I thought my glasses were fogging. When I took them off, the "fog" was still there. The Shekinah Glory was hovering above the music director. He raised his hand high in worship, and it disappeared in the cloud. I was the first one to notice, then Steve. God gave Brother Steve a word once he saw the glory cloud. "I believe that God wants to heal back problems tonight," Steve announced. "Everyone with back problems come to the front." Thirty people were healed that night!

Metal plates and bolts and screws have disappeared in people's bodies, deformities have been corrected and even new organs, such as kidneys, have been received. Five confirmed, new hearts have been reported back to Steve in the last six years along with hundreds of thousand of dollars saved in cancelled surgeries.

Women have shed five dress sizes in one night. This reminds of one miracle that has really stayed with me. It involved a little, bitty, barely twelve-year-old girl. Well, not "bitty." She was grossly overweight.

Steve had prayed over her before. "Brother Steve, I've got to lose some weight. I don't want to go to school because they're making so much fun of me, and teachers won't make them stop."

He said, "Well, we'll pray for you and see what God will do." He prayed for her again, and then he went on to someone else.

I kept glancing over at this child. I watched her shrink! She shrunk to a perfect size and a very cute little girl. When she stood up, her blouse looked like a tent on her, and she had to grab her pants and hold them up with one hand.

Three weeks later, this little girl got up and testified that she lost forty pounds. She didn't diet; she didn't work out. She lost the weight supernaturally. This twelve-year-old caught the fire of the Holy Spirit that night and started preaching and prophesying, which released miracles. People started shedding pounds just by listening to her. Now that's my kind of weight loss program!

On another night I was with Steve, a frail woman in her sixties came to the meeting. Her hair was falling out, she shuffled with a walker and a hose from an oxygen tank forced air through her nose down into her diseased lungs. Cancer was killing her.

Steve prayed for her, and after the prayer, I noticed that she started to move better. Then she didn't need her walker, and I watched her prance around the church. She also disconnected herself from the oxygen.

Three months later, at another meeting with Steve, there was a group of people that gathered to sing up front. I saw a woman join this group and thought to myself that she looked a great deal like the woman who had lung cancer months ago. But this woman didn't have an oxygen hose in her nose or a walker in her hands. She also had a full head of shiny hair.

Steve caught my eye from across the room and mouthed, "That was the dying woman!" She no longer shuffled, but danced. She no longer struggled for breath, but sang! And she looked about ten years younger than her real age.

The doctors confirmed that this woman was completely healed. It was as if she never had cancer in the first place. What a delight!

One final Brother Steve story that just thrilled me involved a young, seventeen-year-old young man who suffered from scoliosis so badly that his back twisted into an "S." Steve prayed for him, and the boy went down under the power of God, falling sideways in slow motion, as if an angel was laying him down.

Finally the young man stood up. His back was completely straight as if given a brand-new spine! He stood about 5'8" with his deformity. After he was healed, I'd say he stood just under six feet. Needless to say, he and his parents went absolutely berserk. Wouldn't you?

This next miracle happened before I even reached Brother Steve's meeting. I was in the parking lot getting some of my books out of my car when a woman approached me with tremendous back and leg problems.

"Would you pray for me in the meeting?" she asked.

I said, "Why wait for the service? What is your problem?" She told me. I said, "Walk for me." She could hardly walk, and every step she took was obviously painful. So I laid hands on her.

I laid my left hand on her shoulder and my right hand on her forehead. I prayed for her, and she about went down on that asphalt. "Now walk," I said. She started walking perfectly. I've seen her again since then, and she always comes prancing by, showing off her walk. That was really a thrill.

⌒◦⌒

I have another Oklahoma story, this time in Tulsa. The room at the hotel was supposed to only hold 200. Somehow, 300 squeezed in. I was up at the front of the room talking when a man stood up and said, "Brother Tommy, we would like to hear every one of your stories, but everybody here wants you to pray for them."

I said, "All of them?"

"Yeah," he said.

He walked up and whispered in my ear, "These are all ministers. Some of them have already left the ministry, and some others are thinking of leaving. They can't seem to get the anointing."

I said, "Oh, come on, that's easy to get."

He said, "Okay. Impart it to them."

I started praying for them, and the fire alarm went off. Well, the hotel staff came and stopped it. I continued praying for quite a few more. The fire alarm sounded again. Once more, the hotel engineering department stopped it.

I was getting close to being through praying and imparting to everyone when the alarm went off for a third time. One of the men asked, "Has this ever happened before?"

The hotel engineer said, "No. We don't know why it keeps going off."

I said, "Well, you've got the Holy Ghost and fire in here. The heat of the anointing is setting it off."

I received a report that after my impartation that day, the ministers who had come out of the ministry returned, and those who were thinking of leaving, stayed. It delights me to think that through my ministry, 300 preachers are still preaching.

This next story involves a very unique impartation that I personally experienced. I was in Los Angeles in 2008 with a local friend named Pastor Kevin Richardson, whose own story is really compelling.

Kevin was a missionary Baptist minister when the power of God grabbed ahold of him. Kevin received the anointing of Brother Seymour when he visited Seymour's grave after two encounters with the Holy Spirit. Now he and another Foursquare friend of mine named Dana Roman brought me to L.A. for meetings. I kept urging them to take me to Seymour's grave. Finally I said, "Dana, Kevin, I want to go to Seymour's grave. I'm not going anywhere else and speaking until you take me to Seymour's grave."

So the next day they took me to the cemetery. Brother Seymour's plot was not well tended at that time, as the dried, dead grass and sandy dirt testified. It was July, and it was hot. I was standing there, sweating. "All right. What now, God?" I said in my head.

"Lie down on the grave," God answered.

"God, do You see how dirty that is and how hot it is?"

Then, louder, "Lie down on the grave." I felt my knees bending.

Before I knew it, I was lying on the hard, baked dirt and feeling like the dead body in Second Kings 13:21. When the discarded corpse fell on the bones of Elisha, the dead man came back to life. As I lay on Seymour's grave, little tingles of electricity shot through my whole body. Finally and all of a sudden, it was over.

I heard God say, "Now you have it." What I now had was Seymour's anointing. I wanted it, so I got it. Just like Seymour wanted what Parham had. Some say, "Oh, I don't believe in that." That's okay. They won't get what they don't want. God's a gentleman. Graciously, Kevin and Dana helped me up and dusted me off. (I took my co-author, Michelle Griffith, to Seymour's grave in June 2012. She had a similar experience of electricity running through her body. Apparently, the "buzz" continued for about half an hour after she got up from the grave. Michelle said she had never experienced anything so powerful and unusual before.)

Dana arranged a meeting for me at a Foursquare church in Riverside. With every speaking engagement, I always let the Holy Spirit bring to my mind what He wants me to say. During my talk at this church, I recalled how Brother Seymour would tell Brother Sines to play a particular tune. He'd start playing it, and Seymour would just walk around for a few minutes and then say, "Now start singing in the Spirit." That meant singing in tongues. The people sang in tongues, and the Shekinah Glory would start rising and thickening until the cloud filled the space and the flames lit up the night, releasing the most wondrous of miracles in the warehouse.

At the end of my time, Dana asked, "Is there anybody who got something from the Lord?"

This young man, about twenty years old, leaped to his feet and said, "Did anybody listen to what Tommy just said? When they started singing in the Spirit is when the great miracles started happening!"

"That's right," I said. "Y'all get up and start singing in the Spirit." I looked at the young man and said, "Obey God. Listen for God to tell you something."

Everyone was singing in the Spirit. Finally he got up and went over to a little girl in the front row who was sick. He prayed for her, and she was instantly healed. They both were thrilled. I love to see people delight in God when they obey Him. God wants to use all of us!

This next story took place at an Assemblies of God church in Augusta, Kansas, where Jim and Tammy Bakker grew up. Thirty-two young people, teenagers, sat in the first row, right in front of me, as I was speaking.

While I was preaching, I kept noticing this young man whose one eye wasn't moving. When I finished, I called him up and asked him about his right eye. "Yes, Brother Tommy, I've got a bad eye."

"Well, would you like it healed?"

He said, "Yes!" So I prayed for him, and he got healed.

I said, "You freely received your healing? Now, freely give."

He asked, "What do you mean?"

I said, "You're going to get all these kids healed. Not me. You."

The young man looked confused. I said, "Didn't you hear me pray for an impartation of the anointing? Now you have the anointing. Get 'em healed."

He looked over at his pastor, and the pastor said, "Yes, go."

The young man looked at me and asked, "What are you going to do?"

I said, "I'm going to go to the back of the room and sit at that table and have a cup of coffee while I watch you get 'em healed. Now, start doing it."

A few months later, I was at a prayer conference in Branson with Billye Brim, one of the members of that church in Augusta came up to me and said, "Brother Tommy?"

I said, "Yeah, how you doing?"

She said, "Brother Tommy, those thirty-two young people in our church were healed by God through that young man. Now there's almost a hundred healed."

This kind of testimony is what thrills me. Not how many I heal, but that I leave something behind, something that remains after I'm gone. That church is having revival.

My first big, noticeable miracle other than raising Brother Silver from the dead, was in 2008 in Troy, New York. I was standing in a checkout line at a local store when I heard two women talking about my upcoming meeting. A man, in his mid-thirties, and his wife and son were also waiting in line. They overheard these two women as well and asked if they could come to the gathering. The women said, "Oh, yes!" and gave them directions. They came.

The man came up and wanted prayer. He didn't want prayer for anything but his wife who wanted to work to make some extra money. She wanted her own business in the location of her choice and to choose her own hours. So he bought her an ice cream truck. Only problem was that the weather wasn't cooperating with selling ice cream. Remember, this is in Troy, New York.

I looked at the man, and I said, "Are you aware that your nose is extremely crooked?" His nose literally lay down on his cheek.

"Yes," he said. "When I was five years old, I had a very violent bicycle accident, and my parents neglected to have my nose reset." So here he was, thirty-something years later with that nose!

"Can you breathe through it?"

He said, "No, I cannot. You'll notice my mouth is always open."

I said, "Okay. Well, let's pray for your wife's ice cream truck." So I closed my eyes, prayed and heard from God. I said, "Tomorrow morning, your yard will be full of kids, and they'll be knocking on your door and demanding to buy your wife's ice cream."

I opened my eyes and looked at him. "Can you look down and notice your nose is perfectly straight?" He looked down. "See if you can breathe through it." He took a breath. He went berserk because he could breathe perfectly. So did the rest of the church. I said no prayer for his nose. It happened sometime during the prayer for his wife. Of course, after that, we had no trouble experiencing miracles. People just started believing.

The next morning he reported back to me that his wife had sold every piece of ice cream they had in that truck. Here's the kicker— she doesn't shut it down now during the winter. She sells all kinds of ice cream during wintertime and makes more money than he does. How do you like that? Go, God!

Down the East Coast in the panhandle state of Florida, I was called to speak at a very special ministers meeting in Jacksonville, originally in the fall of 2009 and then again in March of 2012, by Rev. Valeriana Feliciano of Into the Nations and Gods' House Ministries.

According to Rev. Valeriana, in 2008 the Spirit of the Lord released to her that there would be "a new Azusa" in the future. Having grown up Pentecostal, she knew of Azusa Street, but she didn't know of the hundred-year prophecy...until we spoke on the phone in the spring of 2009 after she stumbled upon my interview on Sid Roth's show, *It's Supernatural.*

The Lord told her to start selling my first book through her ministry to plant the seed of revival in people's hearts. When she started speaking from the pulpit about the stories of Azusa, some saw and felt the manifestation of a thin, misty substance—the Shekinah Glory—fill the air. Then Rev. Valeriana called and made her first invitation to have me speak at an upcoming conference.

The Call to Arms conference in September of 2009 was geared for five-fold ministers in the Jacksonville area. When I told the stories from Azusa, a great move of God was triggered. People were experiencing prophetic words, words of knowledge for healing, and many were having Godly visions. Backs were healed, and there was a great restoration of wearied saints and warriors. Leaders were revived.

In March of 2012, Rev. Valeriana requested that I come again to speak on the last day of another conference. In the middle of my talk, she had one of her most powerful encounters with the Lord to date—definitely her most "public" among witnesses.

Here is her testimony: "While I listened to Tommy, my eyes grew heavy, and it was almost like someone was super-gluing them shut. There was uncontrollable twitching in them. Then the presence of God shot all the way through me and overtook me entirely, rendering my physical body completely limp.

"I started to slip out of my chair when others around me laid me down on the floor. My whole body was shaking as my spirit was taken up. For the first time, I entered the Throne Room of God.

"The Shekinah Glory was made of many colors and sparkled with bits of gold. It was so thick that I couldn't see the Lord. However,

I knew that He was there because we had a conversation. We even laughed together. I was told by those who were observing me on the floor that they could hear parts of our conversation."

That evening, when Rev. Valeriana preached, she was under the "strongest anointing that I've ever had in my life." Just to stand up, she was white-knuckling the pulpit. According to her, "I thought that I would explode, the anointing was so powerful."

One of her friends, who was part of her presentation that night, shot across the room under the power of God, hit a large step leading up to the stage and landed on the floor. The impact of the fall was heard throughout the entire room. The woman should have broken her neck or back, the force was so mighty. The only thing touched was her spirit because there wasn't a scratch on her body.

Rev. Valeriana claims that the anointing lingered for two weeks, evidenced by little sparks of electricity running through her and a lightness in her step as though she was walking on air. She says, "Countless revelations poured out of me like water. When I read the Bible during this time, the words on the pages literally became alive and merged with my spirit."

Rev. Valeriana claims that she has retained some of this heightened understanding of the Word and revelation knowledge to this day.

The hand of God also impacted others during my talk at that conference. One fourteen-year-old boy was saved, then slain in the Spirit where God called him into the ministry. Valeriana's brother, Rev. Gerry Brown, had an out-of-body experience where his spirit hovered right below the ceiling.

Though not everyone saw it, Rev. Valeriana saw another manifestation of the Shekinah Glory. This time it was thicker, "like someone had burnt the toast." In fact, passersby outside the building were unusually drawn and looking in through the bay window.

Is it possible the glory was "misting" around the building as it did at Azusa Street and is now doing in China? We never found out, but this is what I think happened.

Do you remember how God used me to raise Brother Silver from the dead at Pisgah in 1963? In 1998, the following miracle took place at the Wade Street Mission in El Reno, Oklahoma.

Brother Duty, the pastor, invited me to speak. During the song service, I was looking at this lady across the aisle from me. I could tell she wasn't breathing. I got up and preached and looked at her a few times. I finished, and Brother Duty began to close the service down. I thought, "God, when is somebody going to notice this poor woman is *dead*?"

Suddenly, a bloodcurdling scream made me almost jump out of my seat. "Mama's dead! Mama's dead! She's not..." The lady's daughters and grandkids started screaming and going wild and crazy, running around the church.

Brother Duty looked at me, "Do you believe in raising the dead?"

I said, "Yeah, but how can I do anything with all of this mess?"

He said, "Oh, I'll take care of that." He cleared the church and got everybody out but him and me. They had a big bay window in front of the church. Everybody was standing outside, watching.

I said, "Let's get her up. You hold her."

He said, "Okay. But don't take too long. She's not exactly light." I slapped hands on her and commanded her to return from the dead.

She jerked, opened her eyes, looked at me and got angry. She started to slip away again. I said, "No, no, no!" In my head, I was praying, "God, give me something." He did.

I said, "Listen to me, listen to me! You have got a son who is not saved." She stopped and stood up.

"Yeah."

I said, "He's anticipating suicide, and the only person who can talk him out of it is you. You can't die until he gets saved and gets into the ministry. Do you understand me?"

"Yes. Yes, I understand you."

She was the first person whom I got upset with trying to go back to heaven. "You're a prophet," she said.

I said, "No, no, no. I've just got the gift of prophecy."

"I don't care what you got. You're a prophet."

She picked up her purse to leave, then looked at me. "Brother Tommy, I fixed a very good stew. Let's go eat."

I said, "Okay." She waddled off. It seems she came back from heaven with an appetite.

Recalling Pisgah again, I'm reminded of a recent miracle that involved Brother Smith's daughter-in-law, named Ramona. Brother Smith's son, Jimmy, married Ramona, his high school sweetheart. Ramona had a car accident in which she suffered a head trauma and lost her memory.

I sent Jimmy a copy of my first book, and Ramona started reading it. One day I received a call from her. She was anxious. I said, "Ramona, calm down. What's going on?"

She said, "Tommy, I've been reading your book. I didn't even quite get to Sister Carney's story, and my memory has come back. Now I remember everything!" I delighted in that miracle.

I received another call one day and heard a testimony of how God used my first book in a very physical way. This time the call was from a black, retired preacher, who pastored a church in Virginia for over forty years. His son is now the pastor. This preacher wanted to order a new book because he had worn the other one out.

"You wore it out?"

He said, "Yeah, from sleeping with it."

I said, "From doing what?"

He said, "From sleeping with it."

"Why do you sleep with it, brother?" I naturally had to ask.

He said, "Well, every time I'd get sick, I'd want to be healed. The Spirit of the Lord told me to sleep with your book."

I thought, "Wow, okay."

"Now, every time I get sick, I just sleep with the book. I wake up the next morning completely healed." The major healings were his ears popping open and his hearing restored as well as spasms in his leg being healed. Now he'll even sleep with the book for a cold. I believe it's really just obeying God, no matter how odd it sounds—just like Seymour and the box.

One of my favorite stories revealing the release of miracles occurred during a radio interview in the Houston, Texas, area. This brother who asked to interview me had a program on one of the stations in a local radio network. He wanted me to tell some of my stories, and we had fifteen minutes only. He introduced me on air and then turned the mic over to me.

I don't remember anything after that. They said I started telling some stories and, man, I was going to town on them. I came under the anointing is what happened. Well, the network has six radio stations. The owner of the network came by, looked in at me and then turned around and went into the control room. He turned off all the programming on the other five stations and broadcast me on all six. When I finished, I remember saying, "Okay. Now I'm through."

The station started getting calls. Each call was a testimonial of a healing that happened while I was being broadcast.

One woman was in the shower. She had a crippling disease that attacked her legs, and she had to brace herself up just to stand under the water. The radio was on with the volume turned up high because she liked listening to the program. All of a sudden, when I started talking, the feeling started coming back into her legs. God healed her in the shower.

One lady was lying in her bed, paralyzed by some kind of cancer. Whenever she wanted out of bed, she had to have someone come in to get her up. She was listening to the program and started feeling tingling in her spine. She said she was lying there and hollering, "God, what's happening?"

Then she just threw the covers back and got up out of bed, healed. Instead of calling someone for help, she called the radio station with her testimony!

The owner of the radio station was healed of a health problem by just looking in at me while I was storytelling. That's why he turned off the regular programming to broadcast me on all six of his stations. He said he recognized the anointing.

Later he told me that I was the first white man to ever come and speak on their station. I looked at him, his name was Willy, and I said, "Are you sure? Come on."

He said, "No. Blacks in Houston are more prejudiced than the whites. Most of them have a problem." Willy said, "I have a problem with them because I fellowship with anybody, and they don't like it."

Following that broadcast, black people were coming to me at churches where I was speaking, saying, "Brother Tommy, you made a breakthrough in the black community because they don't feel you have one bit of prejudice."

I said, "I don't. Besides that, I can't help it that my color doesn't show."

One woman asked, "What do you mean?" She worked for Trinity Broadcast in Houston. I said, "I'm 1/32 Negro."

She said, "No!"

I said, "Okay...I'm 1/32 black."

She laughed and said, "Are you really?"

I said, "Yes. I am really. Who cares?"

She started shouting and said, "That's good. Who cares?"

Seymour would have been proud.

I remember the saints telling me about an extremely prejudiced man who came to Azusa from North Carolina. At first he didn't get any healing or anointing because of his prejudice. He didn't want any black person laying hands on him.

He went back to his motel, and God paid him a visit. He got his lecture and chewing out from God. The next day he was delivered of his prejudiced attitude. Seymour laid hands on him, and he received the Baptism. He took it back to North Carolina, to an area that became known as Azusa East. He had a tremendous revival there, and the Shekinah Glory was present just as in Azusa "West."

God won't tolerate the wrong attitudes. This reminds me of another story the saints shared with me—this time about Frank Bartleman.

Frank Bartleman lived two blocks from Azusa Street. His wife had just had their son, Johnny, who became my friend and co-worker when I lived at Pisgah. Mrs. Bartleman stayed home to take care of the baby because churches didn't have little nurseries back then. This one particular day, Frank and his wife had an argument before he left to attend services at Azusa Street.

Frank was so many feet from Azusa's door when he ran into something invisible, bounced off it and fell down. Confused, he got up, looked around and started down the sidewalk again. He bounced off the transparent barrier once more. "God, what's happening?" he thought. Well, he made a running charge the third time and hurt himself. "God, what's going on?"

"You were not very nice to your wife," he heard God say. "You want to go in there where God is moving. First you must go back home and make things right with your wife. You were wrong."

God continued to deal with him on the two-block walk back to his house. When he got home, he went down on his knees before his wife. He told her he was the one who was wrong and asked her forgiveness.

Forgiven, he got up and walked the two blocks back to Azusa. This time he walked right through the doors without any interference. His heart was right with God.

❦

"I was naked, and you gave me clothing. I was sick, and you cared for me. I was in *prison*, and you visited me." This passage from Matthew 25:36 calls us to the prisons. I've had a prison ministry for years. My next story takes place behind bars in Stringtown, Oklahoma.

An older woman by the name of Sister Mary arranged for me to get into the prison in Stringtown. She told me that I'd be able to speak in both the lower and the upper parts of the prison.

The lower part is where they brought prisoners who were about ready to be released. The upper part is where the rapists and killers were brought out of their cells. I knew some of them from the prison in Helena. They were on lockdown, and they stayed on lockdown.

The only way they could get out of their cells was to come to church. So, needless to say, everyone in that lockdown would come to church. You had no problem getting them there. The place was full.

I got up and told my stories. When I finished, four prisoners came up to me. The first one was a little Mexican brother. I called him brother because he got saved.

He looked at me and said, "There's something I want to be healed of, but more than that, I want that tongue thing."

I said, "Oh, you want the Holy Ghost."

So I laid hands on him and prayed for him. He started going backwards, speaking in tongues. The prisoner behind him caught him, laid him down and excitedly got up and said, "Okay. I want that thing."

I said, "You want what he's got?"

He said, "Yeah, I want that tongue thing."

I said, "Okay."

He, too, went down, speaking in tongues.

Before I knew it, they were all getting up and getting in line. Whatever the others received, they wanted it, too. Even "the boss," the one who decided who lived and who didn't live, wanted what the prisoners were receiving. The boss had already been saved, but he wanted the "tongue thing." So I prayed for all of them, and they had great revival. Sister Mary was shouting and dancing with delight.

This revival started spreading in the prisons—Boley, Clinton, Helena, Fort Supply, Langston. The prisoners in Boley had tremendous faith to receive their healings. Everywhere I went, the chapels would be packed out.

There was one prisoner in Helena, a big guy about 6'4", who led the choir. Boy, that guy could lead! He had an anointing to lead the song service. The first time I met him, he said, "Tommy, I'm going to see Governor Keating."

I said, "Yeah?"

He said, "I want him to reduce my sentences."

"Okay. Let's pray." So we prayed.

When I came back the next month, I said, "How did you do with Keating?"

He said, "Well, I got a thousand years off."

I stood there blinking at him. I said, "You got what?"

"I got a thousand years off."

"How much time did you have, brother?"

"I had 4,000 years."

"Who did you kill?"

"Nobody. It was all drug related."

"Okay. Well, a thousand years. That's a start. That's twenty-five percent off."

The next month I came to Helena and asked, "Where's Brother So-and-So?"

"Oh, he's at a halfway house in Tulsa."

I said, "No kidding!" The next month I came and asked, "How's Brother So-and-So doing in Tulsa?" "They let him go!" was the answer. Now he's with some big black ministry there in Tulsa, and he's working for the church, leading the choir service. Glory! A 4,000-year sentence reversed!

There was another prisoner who was accepted into Rhema Bible College, and now he's an evangelist preaching all over the place. Another prisoner got into trouble because he had some crooked business dealings. But he got out, and God told him to go into a used-car dealership business. Now he's got three dealerships in San Antonio, and he's wealthy.

I gave the first Hispanic translation of my first book to a Mexican brother who was a prisoner. I called him "Brother Who," because his entire head was shaved except for a little pigtail in the back. He's up in Tulsa now, preaching. From prison to preaching. That thrills me.

I'm going to share one more thing before I tell my absolute favorite story. It's not a miracle, but it just warms my heart.

There's a school about four miles north of Niagara Falls. Several times throughout the year, all of the students—kindergarten through high school—come into the gymnasium and sit on the floor with a few chocolate chip cookies and a glass of milk (some of my favorite things, as you know). The headmaster of the school then sits in front of them and reads from my book. They've had this tradition for almost four years now. They complete the entire book by the end of the school year. This tradition touches and honors me. I hope to visit them one day.

Crossing the continent, my favorite story takes place on the West Coast in Banning, California. This particular church was filled to the brim, full of different youth groups from five churches. This was the first time I was introduced as the "last living link to Azusa Street." This title made me feel pretty historic.

I got up and spoke, and when I finished my stories, I said, "Now, if any of you young people get a word from God to do something, obey Him." This little thirteen-year-old girl, with long, dark hair, came walking down the aisle.

Her pastor's leg was in a cast from a ballgame injury. She walked up to him and laid hands on him. She prayed for him, and afterwards he got up and started dancing around the church. After that, many people got healed that night.

At the end of the evening, I said, "Somebody get the little girl who laid hands on her pastor. Bring her to me." They found her and brought her up front. I said, "Sweetheart, how old are you?"

"Thirteen."

I said, "I want you to listen to me. Did you know that you can pray for healing anytime and anywhere?"

"Anytime and anywhere?"

I said, "Yes." She took that advice to heart.

On the football team, she was what you call the towel girl, the one who runs back and forth handing out towels to the football players. The quarterback got injured pretty badly in the game following my meeting. He was lying there on the field, moaning.

She went up to him and said, "I believe that if I lay hands on you and pray for you, you'll get healed. Do you want me to lay hands on you and pray for you?"

He groaned, "Yeah."

She laid hands on him and prayed, and he was healed. He returned to the field to play. Somebody else got hurt that night, too. She went up to him and healed him as well.

A few games later, if anyone got hurt, the doctor and coach would call her over. "Come here. Come here," they'd say, and ask her to pray for the player. Even the school nurse would call her down to pray for someone in the sick bay.

The school tried to stop her. She was told she couldn't pray for people since it was a public school. She said, "Oh, good. I'm so glad you're trying to stop me. My father said this would happen, and he wants to take this to the Supreme Court."

She asked, "Have you ever heard of Jay Sekulow? Every time he takes one of these cases to the Supreme Court, he wins." She said, "I never just walk up and lay hands on anyone. I ask people if they want me to pray for them. They all say yes. So I'm not forcing them. I have a right, a Constitutional right, to my belief and faith, and you don't have a right to tell me not to. So, thank you. My dad will really appreciate this."

Well, that little middle school thought it over and backed off. It was a public school, but most of the students became Christian because of this little girl.

Now she's almost graduating high school and is having the same results. She continues to pray for people and heal them. There's revival in those schools all because one little girl was told she could pray for healing anywhere and anytime.

This is my favorite story *to date*. I can't wait to learn of new miracles that happen when people read this book. Michelle and I would love for you to share your testimonies with us. Please contact us and let us know how God moves in your lives.

AZUSA STREET—AN INSPIRATION, NOT A DESTINATION

"He causes us to remember his wonderful works." (Psalm 111:4a)

We can look upon Azusa Street as an incredible expression of the heart of God toward His people. Not one who came to 312 Azusa Street was left untouched by His extravagant love. All who came were healed in heart, mind and body. Harmony with heaven filled this small speck on earth.

No one was too young or too old. All were rejoicing children of Abba Father. It was a Divine party, a beautiful, celestial collision of heaven and earth. To re-quote Pastor Bill Johnson, Azusa was a prime example of "heaven invading earth."

The Azusa Street Revival ended in the early part of the twentieth century. However, our God is the same yesterday, today and forever (Heb. 13:8). For this reason and this hope, we are not to park in the past and wistfully look upon that outpouring as something that only belonged to yesteryear like brokenhearted Brother Brown.

We are to live expectantly of how God is going to bathe us in His blessings in this day and time. I like the way Tommy puts it: "We can't get by on what happened at Azusa. We can remember what happened there and know that the same thing is for us." Azusa Street is an inspiration, not a bygone destination.

God is on the move in ways that are to be greater yet, according to the hundred-year prophecy. Global glory, this time! Everywhere! Everyone!

With every keystroke in writing this book, my spiritual appetite has grown insatiable to participate in this move of God, which has already begun in part. I've participated in two miraculous healings to date. Then I think of the Azusa saints performing that many or more in a day for more than three years! In all honesty, at times I've envied the saints and all who experienced Azusa Street.

I hunger for the fullness of this heavenly invasion in my world as I still can feel powerless when I see sickness and death, lack and strife all around me. I've been immersed in the miraculous for months now, daily penning these accounts, while life off of the page still falls short of this glory.

I join others who believe our Christian inheritance is naturally living the supernatural. I've grown a healthy dissatisfaction with a life that is anything less. I want my children dissatisfied with anything less.

"What can I do, Lord? What can *we* do?"

Like Azusa, our role is still to pray it down, fervently filling those heavenly bowls of Revelation 5:8 to the tipping point until we are rained upon again, this time with grander glory and fresh, falling fire, proving the words of Scripture once more: "Nothing is impossible with God" (Luke 1:37). Not a missing limb. Not a body ravaged with cancer. Not a being succumbed to death. Not even an empty bank account.

Complementing this fervor is our resting confidently in God, trusting His promises, His very nature. He was, is and will always be *faithful* to keep His word.

This time, the promised outpouring will not end until the Lord comes again!

APPENDIX

Steve Siler

Mighty Warrior Ministries
PO Box 890742
Oklahoma City, OK 73189
Facbook: Steve Siler
www.StephenSiler.com
email: wheretheeaglesgather@yahoo.com

Rev. Valeriana Feliciano

Into the Nations & God's House Ministries
www.itnmin.org
904-347-5657

Additional Resources

Tommy's Personal Azusa Street Tour with Michelle and Friends chronicles a very special day in June, 2012 when Tommy took me and some friends and family from place to place, giving us his personal tour of the Azusa Street landmarks. The reality style of this piece will make you feel like you were there that summer day. Tommy's plucky personality shines through as he regales us with tales and details of his time with the saints and his personal experiences of today.

This ***Tour*** video brings Tommy and the Azusa landmarks into the homes of people that might never get a chance to hear him speak or travel to these places: *Bonnie Brae, Azusa Street - the site of the mission in downtown LA, the gravesite of William Seymour, and Pisgah where Tommy lived with the saints.* Join us and come along for the ride!

-    BONUS FEATURES include Tommy telling of his visit to heaven along with other stories.

-    Includes a prayer of impartation at the end!

Total running time: 35 minutes

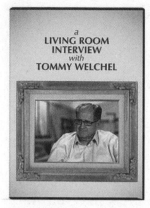

A Living Room Interview with Tommy Welchel...

Kick off your shoes and sit across the couch from Tommy in this comfortable, casual, spontaneous interview. You will enjoy the enthusiastic, natural storyteller as well as the spunky Oklahoma country boy, who reveals his past in his own words to show how God divinely used it to prepare him for his future.

Tommy is waiting for you to join him in the living room where you'll learn more about him and the stories that have impacted the world. It's like having a conversation over coffee with *the last, living link to Azusa Street!*

TRT: 58 minutes

TO ORDER, GO TO:
www.miraclesofazusastreet.com
or
tommywelchelministries.com